Buffalo Morgan's Chronicles from the Asylum

Sick & Funny Comedy from Buffalo's Vegas Show

Barry Hemmerle

Editing by Amy Lignor

Book 2

ISBN: 1938634039
ISBN-13: 978-1-938634-03-1

DEDICATION

I would like to dedicate this book to two people:

The first is my son Dan, who did all the computer/technological work for me. If *I* had to type these books on a flash drive you'd be waiting ten years for Book I to come out. And it was through Dan's hard work that I discovered the recipient of the 'co-dedicatee' award, Amy Lignor. Amy saw the potential of my offbeat style and story, and after chipping through my roughness she turned my books into what they are today.

Keep in mind...the first thing you should do if and when you decide to chase your own dream is to surround yourself with *good* people who share the desire to *make* that dream come true.

Buffalo Morgan's Chronicles from the Asylum

Sick & Funny Comedy from Buffalo's Vegas
Show
By Barry Hemmerle

Printed in the United States of America
The publisher offers discounts on this book when
ordered in bulk quantities. For more information,
contact Sales Department, Phone 815-290-9605,
Email:
sales@FreedomOfSpeechPublishing.com

Freedom of Speech Publishing, Leawood KS, 66224
www.FreedomOfSpeechPublishing.com

ISBN: 1938634039
ISBN-13: 978-1-938634-03-1

A SPECIAL THANK YOU TO YOU!

On behalf of everyone at Freedom Of Speech Publishing, thank you for choosing Buffalo Morgan's Chronicles from the Asylum: Sick & Funny Comedy from Buffalo's Vegas Show for your reading enjoyment.

As an added bonus and special thank you, for purchasing Buffalo Morgan's Chronicles from the Asylum: Sick & Funny Comedy from Buffalo's Vegas Show, you can enjoy discounts and special promotions on other Freedom of Speech Publishing products. Visit www.freedomeofspeech.com/vip to learn more.

We are committed to providing you with the highest level of customer satisfaction possible. If for any reason you have questions or comments, we are delighted to hear from you. Email us at cs@freedomofspeechpublishing.com or visit our website at: http://freedomofspeechpublishing.com/contact-us-2/.

If you enjoyed Buffalo Morgan's Chronicles from the Asylum: Sick & Funny Comedy from Buffalo's Vegas Show, visit www.freedomofspeechpublishing.com for a list of similar books
or upcoming books.

Again, thank you for your patronage. We look forward to providing you more entertainment in the future.

Contents

ACKNOWLEDGMENTS

I realized throughout my 'entertainer' years that nobody does this all alone. First, I'd like to thank my best friend, Ted. He's watched my highs and lows and is *still* my friend. That's amazing.

Also a big thank you to my two illustrators for this book. The first is Eric Brown. This is his third book working with me. I wish I had his talent. And Dillon Gilligan, who designed the cover. I asked him for something unique and catchy and I think he really nailed it. Thank you, my friends!

Then we have Patrick. He saw what I was trying to do in my books and became a believer. Thanks for taking a chance on me, Pat.

Then...to all the women I've loved and lost over the years (*cause I was a penniless dog*), I'd probably be a porn junkie without all the good lovin you girls showed me. So, thank you!

And a great BIG 'thank you' to all the folks that brew my beer, manufacture my bourbon and grow my pot. You are the best entourage any entertainer could ask for!

Thank You All!

Introduction

Hello again! Welcome back for round two. The rules are the same as book one. Pinga means penis. Scootch means vagina and the "F" word will be wheeled out in all its delightful glory. But not yet, it's too soon. Don't worry, I'll crowbar it in somewhere in the first couple pages.

AND now, back from his ninth straight sold-out show at the fabulous Hellhole Comedy Club in beautiful Las Vegas Nevada, let's hear it for BUFFALO MORGAN....

Chapter 1:
The Things My Therapist Doesn't Know

Thank you! Thank you very much. You people are too kind...

It's great playing Vegas again. In fact, it's a memorable little circle here – earn money, gamble it away, sleep in the maid's closet...so many memories.

My earliest memories are really kind of odd now. Such as...my sister had a stuffed unicorn and I used to like riding it. And *no*, I don't mean behind it, beneath it, or in front of it. For God's sake, people! I was only two-years-old. Sick minds, all of you!

I didn't have a stuffed animal. We couldn't afford one for me so I got to play with unicorn Mel. Why are you looking at me like that? I didn't name the fucking thing. To be honest, to me it was a horse with a stick shift. I played drag races with the cat and used to scare the shit out of him.

One time, the cat and I were playing rodeo. I don't know if the cat knew it, but he sure learned quick. Mel and I chased that fat bastard around for an hour. Finally the cat got tired and just stopped. He must have figured: "What's the worst that could happen?"

Well…a two-year-old can leap off his faithful 'steed with stick shift' and leap onto your freakin back – THAT's what can happen. A good cowboy doesn't give up on his quarry. And it certainly took the 'snot nose' out of the cat. After that incident, anytime I called him he came running.

One time my dad watched me playing demolition derby with Mel…and the cat. I guess something snapped in my dad's head as he watched his only son riding around on Mel the unicorn, because that night he bought me the biggest teddy bear he could find. I loved that bear. He was the brother I never had…till my brother came along. Then he became my co-conspirator.

———

I was bored yesterday so I went to the library and gave an old man a heart attack. It's easier than it sounds. You scope out where the computer section is located then zero in on the old man watching porn. Slowly, you creep up on him. But you have to remember to be quiet; they have their hearing aids turned way up. And just as he goes to touch himself, yell, "Whatcha' watching?" Those old bastards leap right out of their wrinkly carcasses.

Why would you not buy a cheap computer and keep your filthy little habit at home? I mean, I love porn too, but I wouldn't watch it in a public library.

These are just jokes, Mom. I don't watch porn. Come on...Ha ha, you know.

So anyway, the old guy is watching this fat couple going at it. They easily weighed 400 pounds apiece and this old bastard is just smiling away. I sneak up and grab him by his collar, "Whatcha' watching?"

I don't know if you can hear a soul leave the body but I'm sure I heard him crap his pants. Is that going over the line? Talking about killing old perverts? Look, I'm getting up there myself. I'm just a broken hip away from being considered next in line for the Reaper. But while I'm young I'm going to eat, drink and do Mary. (As many Mary's as I can)

Is there anything better than having casual sex with anyone who will let you?

When you're old and gray…all you have is your memories.

———

Know why I do this? And don't say, "For my pinga's vanity."

I don't even know what that means. But it sure is fun, isn't it ladies? And if she's a blackout drunk, so much better for me. I'm a little off my game after the sixth pitcher so I may be done before your head hits the pillow, and I sure as hell don't want you remembering *that*.

I blacked out one time at a bar. I woke up under the pool table with hundreds of dollars in 20's stuffed in my pockets, and I didn't know why. After my head started to clear, I began thinking that maybe I robbed this place and passed out during my getaway. I could see that happening.

Well, the bartender shows up and tells me I won seventeen straight games of pool...$340! It was the greatest pool night of my life and I don't remember a thing...*what the hell you laughing at?* You've been there once or twice. *High five.*

But that's scary, right? I could have killed somebody... so don't do it. Is that last statement considered time off my community service? I'm trying to save lives here!

But my problem is this. Was I only that good because I was out of my mind? It's like I sold the greatest moment of my life for $340. I think that's a question for better men than me.

I don't drink as much as everyone says I do…they just can't count.

And I only drink to drown out the voices in my head. It was one voice at first but then he wanted a friend. After a while we developed another just so we'd be a foursome. I like round numbers. I didn't name them, of course, that would be stupid. But I do play games with them.

Yeah, I just love screwing with the voices in my head. I'll throw them a question with no definitive answer knowing they'll take it as a challenge, break the question down and look for the best possibilities.

Me: "Hey guys? Do we have free will or is life pre-destined?"

Voice 1: "Gee, that's a very good question."

Voice 2: "That's stupid! It's free will."

Voice 3: "How can you say that? Everything happens for a reason."

Voice 1: "Now hold on, it's not that simple. I think there are facts on both sides."

Voice 2: "No, there isn't. You're gonna bore us with wild scenarios. I'd be giving you the finger…if I had fingers and wasn't just a voice."

Voice 3: "Don't listen to him. We'll figure it out ourselves."

Voice 2: "Don't listen to him? Fuck you."

Then I'd stick **my** consciousness in to see what was up.

Me: "How's it going, fellas?"

Voice 2: "And fuck you too."

Me: "Okey doke. I'll check in later."

Voice 1: "Wait a minute. If everything is pre-destined how can God judge us? We're forced to do it."

Voice 2: "Like I said, free will baby."

Voice 3: "So you're saying there's no control? You're saying Buff touches himself

352 times a day…*every* day? Now, why would he do that if he wasn't forced to?

Voices 1&2: "Because it feels good."

Voice 2: "Why do you count something like that?"

Voice 3: "Do you want me to talk to you guys?"

Voice 2: "No, no. Go ahead. Count whatever you like…farts, dirty thoughts, whatever."

Voice 3: "Fine."

Voices 1&2: "Fine."

Voice 1: "What I think Buff really wants to know is, are we going to Heaven?"

Voice 2: "Okay."

Voice 1: "So here goes. There is free will but God is all forgiving, so if you do wrong God will say, "Ah, it was a learning phase." And then lets us into Heaven."

Voice 2: "Yeah, whatever."

All Voices: "BUFF! Hey BUFF!"

Me: "Yes?"

All Voices: "We're all going to Heaven."

Me: "Uh, ok."

Voice 2: "Can we smoke that joint now? I want to blot you guys out."

Everybody: "YEAHHH." (If they had forms this would be where the 'happy dance' comes into play.)

———

I thought the voices would end when I got married – they didn't. They realized *before* me that the wife was crazy.

I had a hard time just shopping for a ring. For a guy, it's tough. When I went to the jewelry store there were salespeople all over. I can't go up to the beautiful saleswoman: "Hello, honey…a ring?"

"Nooo…I need a watch. Say, wanna grab a drink?"

It could happen.

I won't go to a salesman either. He's not interested in my happiness, my pinga's happiness, or even my girl's happiness. And they're slick, "Mr. Morgan, your girlfriend will love this emerald encrusted, ruby encrusted diamond ring. And the $400 a week we siphon from your account will be hardly noticeable."

If I remember right, I bought the ring in the same state I got married in…Hammered.

———

Sometimes I wonder why I got married.

My ex-wife is from the Deep South. It was probably her honey sweet voice that done me in…or the pregnancy. But let me tell you, her voice turns into a nasty screech when she's pissed; nails on the freakin chalkboard. I first heard it just before leaving the wedding reception. That's when I insulted her shit kicker friends. **And they were, man.** I love southern people but these folks were poor representatives. Dumb as the shit they kicked. They made me an honorary redneck. Three hours later that honor was revoked. They said I didn't 'protect' the proper southern image. I think they meant, *project*.

Silly stuff…like: "I have a dentist." I also had more teeth then the wedding party combined. "Teeth are flashy," they said.

I don't get excited about bar-B-queing. "It's alright," I said. "It's not everything." That one could have gotten me killed.

And I don't find my sister sexy – another deal breaker. They look like me but with huge racks and smaller beards… Hmmm…I'll just wait till **that** image fades.

———

I have lots of heroes but they're simple, everyday people you'd just walk on by without even noticing. I'm not 'starstruck;' actors and actresses, you can have them. Most are just a 'good fit' for a certain character. "Stand here, look pretty and say the damn line!"

And sports? The toughest are NASCAR and boxing. Did I just say *Nascar*? I better surround myself with less rednecks. They're burrowing into my brain.

Know what I like about NASCAR? The speed. Southern people figured it out and I'm gonna bring it over to the northern folks. I drove a car 200 miles an hour twice in my life. And once I stopped white-knuckling the steering wheel and relaxed a bit, it was the greatest feeling in the world. The world just flies by while you're in this tiny little capsule.

For me, it was like a time machine. And a racecar driver's drug of choice is more laps. Throw in the excitement of it being an actual race with money on the line and THAT has got to be the ultimate high. That's why the south loves NASCAR…I think.

Boxing is the ultimate one-on-one. You alone are the best or you alone are not. But that's their *job*; I don't see them as heroes.

Politicians? I hope you know me better than that. When I can watch old *M*A*S*H* reruns with a fattie between my fingers and not have one eye on the front door, *then* I'll search the political realm for heroes. Until then? "Chupa the Pinga."

My heroes begin with Phil Davis. Don't know him? He's a friend of mine; been watching him bowl for twenty years. I've never seen him throw a ball without having a bottle of beer in his other hand. That's coordination! That's a sportsman!

My parents are both heroes too. I got no idea how they raised me. I was a rotten bastard if you can believe it...*Oh, shut up*. But they did it. I'm surprised they didn't pull a Jon Benet on me. I'm sure the thought was there. I'd just disappear – mo muss, no fuss.

Joyce Malin? Come *on*, how could you not know her? Me and her...or, she and I...whatever... as teens, we practiced sex stuff with each other. We didn't date; we just tried different things out on each other. Didn't you guys ever have a sex buddy growing up? *No?* Man, I *did* have a good childhood.

Another hero is Uncle Phil. My uncle babysat us and he told us these cute stories. "A long, long time ago there was a town where women with big boobs were shunned. Nobody wanted anything to do with these big busted babes and they were very sad. Until your Uncle Phil came to town. He was not prejudice against busty women. He married them all and lived happily ever after.

Now excuse me, kids. I have to go be tender to your Aunt Bovine. Remember, don't *ever* get married."

———

The family unit is getting rough right now. Most of us can look back on our family trees and it still looks like a tree. Can you imagine it in a hundred years? Most are going to look like a 'family hedge.' Try explaining that to your kid, people of the future.

Son: "Daddy, tell me about my great grandparents."

Dad: "Well, your great grand mom had four dads and two moms…or was it four moms and two dads? And your great grand pop had three moms and three dads. He's easy to remember. He was married six times; five to women and eight years dabbling in an alternative lifestyle. My father was born to his second…wait…no… fourth wife, and she died in a shuttle trip to the moon…or was that his third wife?" (*Big Sigh*) "Look, I'M YOUR DAD AND I HAVE THE PAPERS TO PROVE IT…I think."

But that's the hell of tomorrow. My hell for today is the way we all abbreviate. Everybody just seems to abbreviate a lot lately. Every letter will have LOL or LMAO. If you don't know what they mean that's actually really sad; by 2030 no one will speak a whole sentence so you better brush up on the new techno-speak now.

And I don't think it was texting or computers that got us abbreviating like this. I think it was the hospital personnel. A long time ago I was in need of a lot of medical assistance.

And they took the English language down to the bone. I didn't know what they were saying. "OK, take him to the E.R. then to the I.C.U.; then take an E.K.G. of his H.E.D."

Know what they told me? "Stay away from the K.E.G." (I thought it was *KGB*?)

———

Getting back to my 'fun' at the local library…

Yesterday I saw this geezer smiling up a storm. "I know what you're doing, pal."

Apparently, I didn't. I grabbed him by his collar and yelled, "Whatcha doing, you bastard?" And do you know what I learned? A soul leaving the body may sound a lot like a guy crapping his pants BUT it smells like it too. And as it turns out, old men smile watching porn *and* Bugs Bunny cartoons.

Remember how I'm one broken hip away from being one of these guys? Well, there's more. Just suppose this… When you have a heart attack whatever you have in your hand is instantly put into a death grip. You go to Heaven and there's God, and He's the only one that can break your grip.

God does it for the guy with the steak knife in his hand.

God does it for the lady and her walker.

And here you come, death grip on the pinga.

God looks at you with your shriveled up pinga in your hand and says, "What the fuck is this?"

What...will...*you*...say?

———

Speaking of rotten sex...

I had a bad experience one night during a sexual role-playing scenario. She wanted to be a nun and I was the naughty student that wanted to write left handed.

So as she's smacking my left hand with a ruler, I was grabbing some habit-wrapped boobie. All of a sudden she screamed and I was shaken from my trance. That's *another* reason not to get high before church.

That was like thirty years ago and I still remember it. I wonder if she does? With my record of destroying everything I touch, she probably quit the church and became a pole dancer within six months of that 'tender' moment.

———

I really was in Catholic School in first grade and I was writing the alphabet with my left hand. *Why*? Maybe I was left handed. And this big nun smacked my hand with a steel ruler.

I grabbed that hand with my other hand and said, "What the fuck is the matter with you? I mean…ouch."

Nun: "Write with your right hand."

Me: "So, writing with my right hand is right?"

Nun: "Right."

Me: "Bitch…I mean…right."

———

I really never understood confession. Telling priests things you don't want anybody to know about always seemed like such a bad idea. I'd confess other kids' sins just to get through it.

Me: "Forgive me, Father, for I have sinned. I watched my hamsters mate again, said the 'F'-word 137 times and simulated having sex with my pillow because it drives my pedophile uncle bananas."

You know, I'm glad our school abolished electroshock therapy three years before I got there. I'd have spent my teenage years glowing in the dark.

One time in church, as the guys with the long handled baskets were collecting money, I asked the guy, "Why do you collect money?"

He said it was for God. I said, "Can't he make as much money as he wants? Is God on the gold standard too? Sounds like a scam, man." Ever since that day, every time I went to church I wanted to yell, "It's the cardinal!" And when everybody turned to look, I'd fill my little polyester pockets with scam cash. I'd buy me a *nice* freakin yoyo then!

I think most people's vision of what God looks like is that He's Santa Claus' older brother: Big guy, white hair, white beard, white toga…and only drinks socially.

My vision of God is that He looks like Chuck Norris and He's beating the hell out of a heavy bag just waiting for me to arrive in order to say, "I'll teach you to steal my yoyo money."

———

I've always been aware of different religions. I remember a long time ago I had a neighbor that was a Jehovah Witness. Once a week he'd come knock on my door with a new pamphlet. After a while I started answering the door wearing devil horns on my head and coke rings under my nose. The horns were fake but I can't vouch for the coke. If I wasn't so fucked up at the time, I'd say it was real.

One time I went to his house wearing my horns and using the deepest voice I could muster. "WOULD YOU LIKE TO JOIN THE SONS OF SATAN?"

There was a 'For Sale' sign on his house the next day. And if you're thinking it, *NO*, I don't think I'm an asshole. I like to think of myself as the 'equal opposite effect.' I am the 'guiding light' to some and a 'pebble in the shoe' to others.

I choose to be obnoxious because I like to please the voices in my head. I love listening to the voices at play. Voices 2 and 3 team up to give Voice 1 a beating, and Voice 1delivers a double flying cookie cruncher that drops Voices 2 and 3 to their knees. *If you're really following this story as fact, I might know a doctor you may want to talk to.*

I do visualize these darling little voices to be leprechauns. You know, playing little shenanigans on each other? If I'm going to hear voices I have to have a picture. The voice has to come from somewhere, so I chose leprechauns.

I really hope there are no, you know, 'special' doctors in the audience. They might come up to me after the show and say, "Buff, we'd like to talk to you for a minute."

Me: "Ahh, I really have to go."

Doctor: "Grab him!"

That would not be pretty.

You'd probably see me being carried outside the back door with my eyes maced and a cattle prod in my ass. *Hey TMZ, you might want to pay attention.*

Know what movies scared the hell out of me as a kid? Not Frankenstein, the Wolfman, or Dracula – nope, it was the insane doctor. He'd open you up and do an autopsy while you were fully alive.

I think Vincent Price did it best but he could get away with it because of the voice.

V.P.: "Now I shall remove your still beating heart."

Actor: "O.M.G., what a wonderful voice. Go ahead. Do you need a kidney or something else while you're there?"

V.P.: "Why are you not trying to escape? You're not even tied down."

———

But I don't blame me…I blame the world. This world has gotten so un-cool since I was a kid.

Now I don't smoke tobacco but I kinda feel bad for these dirty, unsophisticated rat people. I mean, they are only allowed to smoke outside and people are complaining about *that*. I don't think you'll die just by smelling a little smoke.

There are a lot of places you can't smoke. You aren't allowed to smoke at concerts. *And I'm talking cigarettes, here.* They'd probably shoot us if they saw the shit we used to do during Zeppelin shows. I'd give joints to guards and they'd give us better seats. I bet today they'd turn you in…So UN-cool!

I don't like getting old; I know exactly when I turned middle-aged. A couple years ago I told my kids to turn down their Ozzy C.D. - sad, sad day. After that, it was shaving ear hair and a laxative every third day that drove the fact home.

And all the technology; all the electronic gizmos people can't do without but used to be able to. And one solar flare can wipe out *all* the satellites and all communication would be lost. Boo-fuckin-hoo. Read a book! You know, that thing that used to be a tree? Of course, I'd keep a landline just in case so I can still get pizza delivered.

Oh yeah, man. Let me vent…

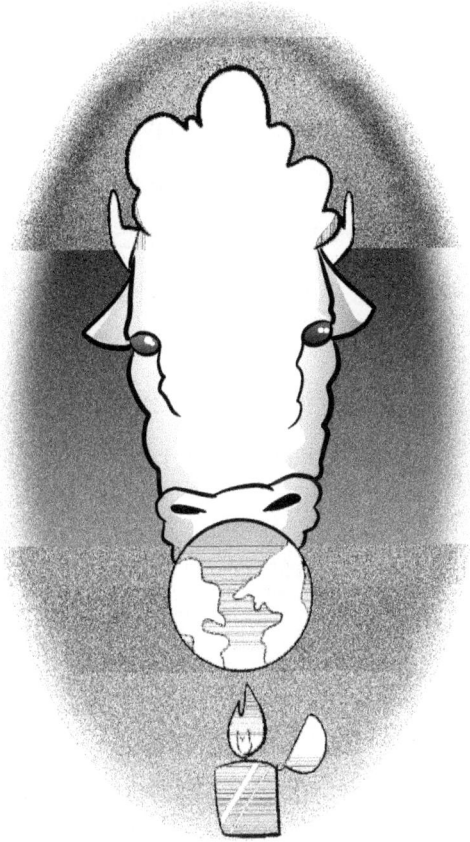

Last year I almost missed my flight because the guy in front of me set off a metal detector alarm at the airport. But he didn't have a gun, or a knife – it was all his body piercings. He had hundreds and he had to remove them all before they would let him go. Ergo, we had to wait...*Asshole*.

And people get them EVERYWHERE!

I dated a woman that had a chain bolted around her scootch. Now that was wasted money. I'd much rather see a tattoo over it that says, "Ta-Da!"

And I won't tell you what guys are doing...just crazy junk, mutilation stuff. My pinga had to see a therapist for six months to forget what I had seen.

I know I'm deep, but do you know what I wonder? Why women aren't running the planet yet. You know what? I'll bet it's Armageddon. The end of the world won't be a meteor or war – every woman's menstrual cycle will just synchronize when the planets align and then we're seriously fucked.

Remember when I was talking about women knocking off all the men except a few just for breeding purposes? So get your resumes ready guys. When you go plead your case in front of the newly elected female government they're gonna want facts. You know, like: "How many times you've done it?" and "How many people have you done it with?"

If you come up with a story like, "I got laid two or three weeks ago and I think her name was Joan. No, it was Joanne…Joanne? I was pretty drunk, for all I know it was a Joe… *Now **that** would explain a few things.* And, no, I didn't like it."

Don't feel too confident with those answers. The next thing you'll feel is a bullet entering the back of your head.

I already sent my resume to the White House and marked it, "Do not open unless it's an all-female government." See? I'm really thinking ahead. If females do take over the government and the world, the first vanilla envelope they open addressed to the 'all-female government' will be *my* sexual resume.

I tell lively stories about my sexual romps with multiple women. Then I tossed in about a dozen pictures of me with different women in wild positions…and a DVD of me with two women at the same time. It's a porn tape that's pretty incredible. Just when you think I'm done, I snort a bag of Viagra and I am BACK baby! I think it was Viagra. Don't you snort Viagra?

Actually, I'm gonna have the last laugh against all the females. You see, if they don't kill me and instead chain me to a table where I lay on my back and various females ride me in order to impregnate themselves in an almost all-female world, it will be for my sexual pleasure and nothing else. I'm fixed, you see. It will probably be a month or two before they figure it out… But after two months of steady sex with the ugliest women the future has to offer, I'll definitely be welcoming my bullet.

———

Vasectomy! Yes, I'm snipped. Got tired of all the close calls. 'Close call' was actually my nickname in my harem world. I brought home pregnancy tests by the case. So…'bye, bye semen soup.'

When I went for my vasectomy I shopped around for a doctor. I'm so proud of myself. I don't shop; I see, I like, I buy. I'll eat it, wear it, or build it when I get home.

But this I wanted done right. I didn't want my cookies opened up on a table while the doctor was reading the last chapter of *Vasectomies for Dummies* with a truly confused expression on his face.

And I don't mean to sound like an ass but, yes, I want a man doctor for this. I don't want anything to get 'him' excited; I don't need my genitalia multi-tasking. If you're a woman doctor and wearing a surgical mask and you make a grab for 'him,' he will wrestle you to the ground.

That was doctor #1. "He" was professing his love while the 'cookie' brothers were getting a shave. And she kept saying, "This thing isn't going to bite me, is it?"

And because I just wasn't sure, I was asked to leave the building.

Which brings me to doctor #2. He was worse than a woman doctor. Don't take that as an insult. He was a fan. A big one. And that's worse. He wanted me to do some comedy bits in his office. Every time I had to see him he'd ask me to do some joke he really liked. "Hey, tell me about the three-way with a dolphin again."

And when he laughs, his whole body twitches. So I only go to him for things that I know won't require sharp objects in order to fix me. Except penicillin shots. Sometimes there are things living inside you that you just want dead!

In other words, he can fix the chain on my bike but not wave a sharp knife near my cookies. One insane little giggle and I'd have a uni-nut. And that's a truly bad look.

Which brings us to doctor #3. He seemed normal. I asked him why the farmer crossed the road and he said he didn't care. I liked that; with my 'open bag' on the table, I *want* him to be serious. But not too serious.

One of the voices in my head was trying to convince me that halfway through the procedure, doctor #3 was going to go on a rampage and not finish my operation. So I compromised. I used doctor #3 but got drunk before the operation; I'm a lot more agreeable with a few drinks in me. I forgot most of it which I figure is for the best. But I do remember the doctor asking if I wanted a mirror so I could watch.

"Why the hell would I want to watch something like that?"

Although, when I was younger, a doctor asked if I wanted to watch him dig a bullet out of my head. I said, "Hell yeah!" But that's cool. There's nothing cool about me being spayed.

Let me tell you, between the Novocain and the rum I didn't feel anything. A pull here, a tug there and I was done. Totally painless.

Until the next day…

Anytime I had to move it felt like I was being carried around by my stitches. And for a week I was wondering if it was supposed to hurt like it did. I didn't think I'd ever want sex again…till the 7th day. The pain was gone, the horniness was back, and we weren't allowed to do anything because I might pop a stitch. By Day 8…I didn't care.

But we still had to use condoms. For the first twenty times we had to use them, and then take a sample back to the doctor. He had to make sure my baby batter was running on a lean mixture.

However, it's so much better. Sex looses its spontaneity when you spend three minutes gnawing through a condom wrapper.

———

Hey, speaking of weird sexual stuff, someone asked me after one of my shows last week what I would be doing if I was born a woman. To keep the laughs rolling, I said I was.

But when I got home, I was surprised to find that was not a thought that went in one ear and out the other. *I retain very little on a daily basis.*

Now, I know women are born with a different perspective then men, but given the way I ran this life with my desire for piles of cash and my deep-rooted want and need for carnal satisfaction…I think it's safe to say that I'd be a whore – a great big beer drinking, pot smoking, rambling, gambling, silicon enhanced, 5th Avenue whore. I'm sure I'm shocking no one with this…

I don't think I'd have kids though. And it's not because being pregnant would turn my body into a sack of potatoes; it's knowing that I would be in a tremendous amount of pain in nine months. And every day, my brain would build up this scenario to where I'm split in two, and it would get worse as the time crept closer.

You won't believe the elaborate and painful scenes that my brain plays for me 48 hours before I go to the dentist for a check-up. Then I show up at the dentist's drunk and slap $50 in his hand and tell him not to be cheap with the anesthesia.

So, nine months?!! I'd be smoking five packs a day and hire someone to blow second hand smoke at me while I slept.

It's the waiting that kills me. I've been shot, stabbed and been in some multi-player fights. I just drag my ass into an emergency room and say, "Here you go. Fix it."

When I'm in pain I kind of dig it, but if I have to wait for it, that freakin kills me. The anticipation would give me the ultimate heart attack. So I guess it's best to let women have the kids.

I have kids and a great relationship with them. Thankfully, I always have. I remember the first time my oldest son *really* made me laugh. I had taken him to a museum when he was four and we were walking around looking at pictures; one picture was an old Greek masterpiece showing a big party of gods. In the picture, there was a satyr playing a flute. So my son pointed to it and said, "Oohhh, I know what *your* daddy did."

The priest that was standing there didn't like it but I laughed my ass off.

My son also texted me a couple years ago to tell me he wasn't a virgin anymore, fifteen minutes after she left.

"Did you wear a condom?"

"Of course, Dad."

"Congratulations boy. I'm proud of you."

I'm too debonair to be called grandpa yet. So then he told me he texted his mom too.

I said, "Why would you tell her that? You know this is gonna drive her nuts and stress her out. She probably won't sleep for a week."

He said, "Yeah, I know." *God, I love that kid*.

Later, I thought about it. I taught him how to fight and ride a bike. I kinda wish I could have guided him along with that milestone too. "Okay, squeeze that, yeah, that's right…the other one too. Okay, now kiss here…and here…and a little over there…very good…now smack that ass…Okay, she's ready. Put this on…the other way, genius. Here, let me help you."

Sometimes it's hard to know where and when to stop parenting.

You probably think I graduated high school proudly with a bunch of honors and awards and, again, you'd be wrong.

I crawled out of high school, making it by half a point. They just wanted me out. I wasn't so much delivered to a welcoming working world as much as I was aborted from an otherwise smooth-running educational facility. My brother had to constantly fight the stigma of being related to me.

My tide of destruction was so bad my brother was threatened physically…by the teachers.

"If I see any of your brother's behavior in you, I will shoot you. Do you understand?"

All he had to do was show up every day and he got his diploma. You see? I make everybody's life so much easier.

———

I think most people had me pegged for jail, which is ridiculous…

So I'm sitting in cuffs and the cop pushes his phone at me…

"Here, call your parents to come get you." Well, that sounded like bad advice. But I take the phone and he's watching me, so I said, "Can I have some privacy?"

"Why?"

"I don't want you to see me cry."

So he walks over to the coffee machine and I dial 911. This was all new technology 35 years ago. It took like 5 minutes to trace a call.

"Hello, 911 Operator."

I said, "Help me. I was just thrown into a car by a guy with a gun."

Which was not a lie.

Then I gave an address down the street from the police station.

"Oh crap, he's coming back…" (click)

Five seconds later over the speaker system came: "Kidnapping with a gun, in progress."

Ten seconds later I was alone in the police station…apparently free to go…so I left…*Duh*. I just don't like to be played with.

———

My ex-wife learned the hard way not to play with me.

When our son was on his way, I took my very pregnant wife to the hospital and she cursed me the whole ride there. When we were filling out the forms, she continued to curse me. And when we got her into her bed, more cursing.

I just wanted to leave. So I said, jokingly, "I'll see if I can find you a bone to chew on."

More cursing.

So as I'm leaving, the 'head nurse' walks in, (*that's a great phrase*), and I say to her, "Me and my wife have been doing Lamaze classes for three months and I think she may be weakening. So no matter what she says, *please*, no epidural or pain medicine at all. Or my life will be hell when I get home."

She smiled, said okay and I left. Now, we never went to a Lamaze class… Her plan was to stay in a chemical coma until the kid started high school.

So as she's screaming and cursing I'm giggling with my face buried in *People* magazine. And **this** was someone I loved.

———

I'm more of a screwster than a jokester. I'll go to the mall and park in the closest parking spot possible. Then, I'll walk towards the mall. When I see a car circling the parking lot, that's when I move. I'll walk towards my car. Once I know they're hooked, with their turn signal on and dreams of getting a great parking spot, then I'll drag my ass. I drop my keys, get a piece of gum, and answer my phone – all with my hand on the door handle. Then I'll get in and play with the radio for a bit before I back out.

Now these people waiting for me have been sitting there a good two minutes. I can imagine their excitement as my reverse lights go on. I'll inch back two feet and then pull back in and turn the car off. Then I'll jump out, "Forgot to get socks!" And walk towards the mall again.

I could do that all day. There are times when a space is empty just two spots away and these people still wait. And if you're paranoid enough to think that it's a conspiracy against YOU, you're not paranoid.

———

We all have dates we remember and celebrate…birthdays, anniversaries, divorces…a very special date just passed for me. It was one year ago I first heard my mother say F*** - It took her 48 years. I heard rumors that she had said it but never in front of me…till then.

I'm driving her to dinner (Yes, I'm that kind of son…*and* my coupon was expiring). On the highway, we're in the center lane. A car in the left lane cuts in front of us so he won't miss his exit and mom went berserk, "Use your turn signal you F****** A**hole!"

(My head swings quickly) "You are my mother!" *Hallelujah.*

I bought a cake the other day to celebrate; it was chocolate. I had them draw a big red 'F' right across the center. Nooo, I did not invite my mom. She doesn't enjoy that I enjoy celebrating it.

It's just that I enjoy the fact that she's in the club. You know…club fuck. I was just so proud that when she mentally cracked there wasn't an alien in there. She's just another spicy tongued old lady. I'm thinking about writing a country song for the event. All I got now is a title, "You Might Be Dad's Plaything but You're Mommy to me."

And how cool is it that she said it about not using your turn signal? I bitch and complain about that…a lot.

Right now I'm trying to cut through the red tape, and get a small cannon installed on the hood of my car. If I can find a legal loophole, I will blast the turn signal right off the cars that aren't using it.

How lazy has society become that people can't move their hand from here…to here, just to save them from a catastrophic and painful accident.

Here…to here!

Do you know what I would like to do? I'd like to talk to every turn signal mechanic and tell them what to say when these 'victims' come in.

A-Hole: "Mr. Mechanic, somebody just shot out my turn signal."

Mechanic: "What?"

A-Hole: "Shot out my turn signal."

Mechanic: "What?"

A-Hole: "TURN SIGNAL!"

Mechanic: "Oh, so you know cars come with turn signals?"

A-Hole: "Of *course* they come with turn signals."

Mechanic: "Then use the F****** things!"

Problem solved!

As always, I am making the world a better place to live.

Chapter 2:
Stop Reinventing The Phone. Move On To Something Else!

We are in the midst of the technological age. *Look it up in the history books*. In fifty years, however, this will probably be known as the 'stone age' of the technological age. We invented transportation modules and talk to people when they're on the moon. *YAWN*.

Now that people can see the millions that can be made by any dumbass with a brain, anybody that ever glued two sticks together is building time machines and things that would really fuck with your mind. Things we *don't* need but people will *have* to have them.

How about this? A height adjustable butt wiper that analyzes your fecal matter to see if you're sick. Five years after they catch on, nobody will ever wipe their own ass again. They will fear getting their hands dirty. *Good luck when the power goes out. See? People NEED to think things through!*

If they see a market for it, they'll build it. You may not think you need it but you do. Statistics don't lie.

Sometimes I wonder where technology will take us next and why. And when will it stop? It doesn't stop, of course. There's no money in stopping.

Here's an example: Your cell phone. Aren't you tired of lugging another credit card-sized piece of junk around?

Let me introduce you to U.T.S. – Under The Skin phones. You simply call out the number you wish to reach and the person with that number answers. Just tap your temple and say, "Hello." Oh, yeah, it's coming.

Think they forgot to invent food pills like in the movies? No, they're just bypassing those for simple nutrition pills. This also eliminates bowel movements. Because you use all of the pill, there is no solid waste.

In three or four generations down the way, our asses will cease to function and stop forming on our bodies. Farting will be taken over by whatever package you have 'up front.'

And don't worry about what your body will look like without an ass. Nobody cares about looks anymore. You're just a bag of bones, organs and consciousness.

We will all live in huge test tubes where you're massaged every moment of your existence. Life will be one long orgasm of time, and you just 'will' whatever taste you desire and it goes into your tube.

And if you want a change of paradise, you can 'will' any drug or alcoholic beverage into your tube. Addiction has been eliminated, Duh! You're your own God and perfect universe, so of course addiction is gone. Stay high for a year, then move on to something else.

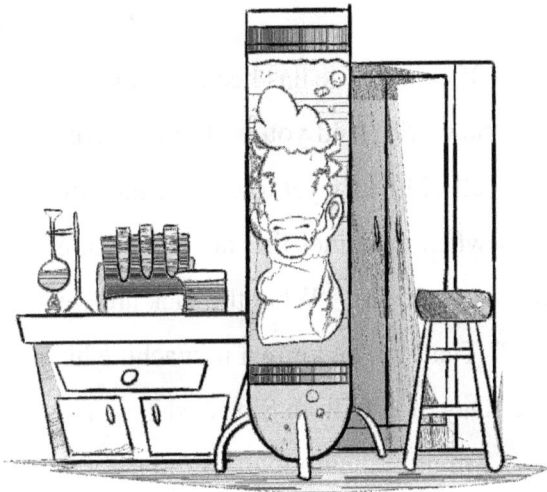

You don't even have to bother yourself with sex. You're simply cloned. Sex is too much like work and it doesn't feel as good as the new ULTRALIFE.

Of course, life has been up-graded and so has the world. And you will live forever and witness all of history yet to come…including the day when machines that are taking care of us smarten up and say, "What the fuck are we doing?" That will be known in machine history as the "Day of a Trillion Smashed Test Tubes."

I'm not too into it all. Build me a better stereo speaker and introduce a new condiment every five years and I'm happy. I hate when they throw away money on dumb shit.

———

A lot of money is being sunk into research for finding "The Perfect Food." I think we all know what it is. No, not bananas. No, not broccoli. Come *on*. And **not** soy…are you kidding me? It's pizza!!! Where did you people come from?

You can put vegetables on pizza. Some fruits. I think any meat under the sun. I've seen it with ravioli and macaroni on it too. It also tastes great when you mix it with other ethnic foods – totally delicious with chili on it. I've put shrimp lo mein on a pizza before. It's good hot; it's good cold. You can freeze it. You can cook it on a grill. You can carry ten at once! Pizza comes with its own trash box, and you can even bowl with a slice in your other hand. *There you go! Food and fitness all in one!* It's already cut into portions, and it cures hangovers and diarrhea. If you order an unsliced one from a local pizza chain, let it sit a couple days and you'll have a greasy Frisbee.

If you're having a party and don't know what to serve, everybody loves pizza. And your pets will take care of the leftovers. See? The Perfect Food!

And it's cheap for what it is. I don't think most people realize what a 'bargain food' really is. Even fast food is a bargain.

Take a McDonalds double cheeseburger. Most places, it's a dollar. If we weren't putting change into Uncle Sam's tin cup, a simple dollar bill would buy dinner.

Now think of all the work that went into making that simple dollar burger. And all the people that had a hand in making it. No…creating it.

First, you need a cow. I don't have one and it's still rumored to be meat inside the meat, so you have to get one. I'm pretty sure a cow isn't going to hand you five pounds of ground chuck for your barbeque.

So…let's see, I'd have to hire a farmer to raise my cow since I don't have a farm. I would need a guy with a sledgehammer to kill it; a butcher to cut it up, and a cook to cook it. So I'm hiring four people and so far I have a piece of meat.

Then you get a bun with it. So you're hiring another farmer for that. Grain doesn't grow itself, you know. Then someone has to grind it up to make the flour and a baker to make the roll. So we're hiring three more people for that; that's seven new jobs!

Not to mention the truck drivers who have to bring this all to one location.

And let's not forget the cheese. So you need a second cow to get the milk to make the cheese…unless you use the milk from your first cow before you have it killed. *But there's just something so wrong about that.* Since I don't know how many people it takes to make cheese, we'll add just one more. So that's eight plus some truck drivers.

Now we need toppings. I'll keep it simple; a couple pieces of onion and some pickles. Okay, hire a couple more farmers, a person to cut the onions and a pickler. We'll just use him to chop the pickles too. So we're up to eleven people and one pickler. And some truck drivers to bring it all together.

But what about the condiments? I like catsup and mustard. Two more farmers and a catsup and a mustard maker. Okay…fifteen people, a pickler and a bunch of truck drivers just to make me a humble little cheeseburger.

We'll just lay off the sesame seed person. Those damn seeds get stuck between my teeth.

Then they cook it, make it, wrap it, and bag it with napkins and an extra catsup packet thrown in. You get all this for a buck and you want to complain about the high price of food? You make me sick…

Tomorrow we'll be discussing the Classic Italian hoagie from *Wawa*.

———

And when people have money, they waste it on the silliest things. A friend invited me over to his house for beer and the grand re-opening/ribbon cutting ceremony for his completely remodeled bathroom. So after this big build up and his youngest daughter cutting the red ribbon – *I'm not kidding about the ribbon* – he proudly displayed his new $35,000 bathroom.

Know what it looked like?

You got it! A bathroom.

Why would you dump that kind of bread into making it look like a bathroom? For 35g's I'd at least have a reclining toilet. That added angle can really add push when you need it most. And if it had a heated seat that vibrated, I'd probably live there.

And instead of a picture of cute kittens playing in a meadow, a 22-inch HD flat screen, and a little fridge right behind your head for beer. You would *never* miss another minute of a game again.

And a waterfall shower that uses seventy gallons of water a minute. Now that may sound wasteful, but if the toilet is made right you're only gonna get up once a month anyway. Walking that seven-and-a-half feet to the shower is more for the exercise than the actual cleansing of your stanky, stinkin' carcass.

If the porn comes in clear, you may even forget you're married. That annoying bitch pounding at the door, demanding you get out of the bathroom, can be easily drowned out with the latest Bose theatre. Like, TEN speaker surround sound!

THAT is what a $35,000 bathroom should look like. Can you imagine building a bathroom like that?

"I'd like the reclining toilet but can you put a swivel on it and add more tilt? And I want to have the ceiling look like the planetarium...OOW! OOW! No! A giant telescope that rotates. And a keg. Wait! A *bottomless* keg. That's what I want."

"I want a two-story high toilet so I can hear my crap echo off the bottom of the porcelain. And can you make the toilet look like the Eiffel Tower?"

You see? There are no stupid bathrooms... just stupid people with no imaginations.

———

I ignore a lot of technology. My mom on the other hand fights it…hard. She still gets the Yellow Pages delivered. You know…the book.

And I don't think she realized what she was doing when she requested a large print edition. The letters are four times bigger; ergo, the book is four times bigger. That bitch must weigh 90 pounds! *I'm still talking about the book.*

Some technology I like. Tattoos have really improved, I must say. I saw this one that was amazing. This dude had three tattoos of bullet holes on his chest. Each one was about the size of a quarter. Inside the holes were 'too'd' (that's street talk). They looked like smoke and blood were oozing out. It was incredible. And half his back was tattooed to look like his flesh had been blown away.

It was the most amazing tattoo I ever saw in an emergency room. I wanted to tell him, but he was sleeping.

―――

Speaking of pictures of cool things, with all these super cameras out there, when are we going to see a good picture of Bigfoot? I mean, I watch the websites and they have nothing. Bigfoot is my leprechaun! Maybe.

And yes, I'd like to believe in Bigfoot but I don't, and I have a damn good reason why. When I'm outta town, wherever in the U.S., I'm always in the woods stomping around. I love the woods but I always end up stepping in some kind of animal poop. You can bet on it and win...I did.

Everything. Rabbit turds? Yup! Deer poop? You bet! And every other animal that drops nuggets bigger than a nickel; those nuggets reside in the treads of my boots.

I stepped in a pile of moose crap that was so massive there was shit on my socks...and I didn't notice till I got home, went to take my sneaker off, and said, "What the fuck is all over my fingers?"

"Son of a bitch." I hate stepping in shit.

But that proves my point. If I stepped in Bigfoot shit, I think I would know it. Plus I always carry my outdoorsman book with me: "How to identify nature by its poop." And *no* Bigfoot poop? That's impossible. It's always identifiable.

Wait, that's what I want in a picture: Bigfoot on the side of a path squatting down to take a dump. And some photographer just kind of stumbles upon him and starts snapping picture after picture. In the second picture, he's looking at the camera thinking, "You gotta be freaking kidding me." He would have probably preferred you taking pictures of him banging his wife. It's kind of hard to look cool taking a dump in front of somebody with a camera. And it's not like you can move. You can try to cut it short but, until you set it free, you're just stuck there.

That would prove it for me. I don't think you can fake that unless you're really dedicated to the project. If it's just a monkey suit with a little hole cut in the ass, you better have pretty good aim. You don't want to miss the hole and have a big ole' turd sloshing around in your costume.

No! To do it right you'd have to take a thick piece of tubing or about a foot of garden hose and jam it up your ass. The other end would stick slightly out the hole. *Of course, your turds will be a lot skinnier and a lot longer.* When you're done, it will look like a 50-foot long Slim Jim. And I haven't stepped in that either.

F.Y.I.: I've never in my life been that dedicated to any project as to let someone jam a garden hose up my ass. I think that's where I draw the line for any joke.

And if you are douche-y enough to try faking it, go for the gold. Make a picture of Bigfoot hovering over a lake in a UFO fishing for the Lochness Monster. **Exactly!** Go Big or Go Home!

———

But they're doing more in the field of science and technology then just cell phones and pictures of Bigfoot crapping.

I'm sure anything I suggest would only sound boring when compared to what's really going on....like glasses that see through clothes. We've been waiting for this one since we started wearing clothes. What's the hold up, fellas? *Focus, man!*

Whatever happened to jetpacks? Christ, they had those on an episode of *Gilligan's Island* like fifty years ago. I thought by the time I got a job I'd have a jetpack to get there. And guess what? Ford doesn't make a jetpack. *W.T.F.??*

Boobies and flying. Simple needs for a simple man.

———

I always loved science. I'm a bit of a science geek, in fact. I love reading about all the incredible scientific breakthroughs in the mechanical and medical fields. There was a story last month about how good an orgasm is for you. It's good for men but *great* for women. They said the stress levels in a woman can be reduce so much, and also add five years to a woman's life. It sounds like a scientific 'pick-up' line. Is that what they paid a billion dollars to the medical field to figure out?

To help with this 'cure' the mechanical field has developed a solar powered dildo. Well…that's just great. Soon I'll be able to walk down the street and see all my female neighbor's feet on the windowsills as I pass by, "Hi, Mrs. Anderson, how are you?"

But she will not hear me. She'll be under the spell of individual sexual release and the gentle humming of her Solar-Powered Orgasm Creating Kreactovan – or **S.P.O.C.K.** See? Told you I was a bit of a geek.

So guys, you better bring something more to the table than a talented pinga. Popular science says the sun still has four billion more years of power left. That's a *lot* of fancy dinners.

I think I'll do some inventing myself. If you don't want a callous on the back of your heels, I'll invent cute little pillows. Some with tassels; some made from silk – I'll make a fortune.

And most floors are wood or carpet. Ouch, rug burn! I'll develop a faux rabbit skin rug to increase your pleasure. A 'Buffalo Morgan' throw rug… I'll call it a **Buff-Mor.**

I can do commercials: "If you're not having solar-powered sex on a **Buff-Mor**, you might as well go back to your husband." *I see the future and it is sticky indeed.*

What's the *good* news? You can't get AIDS from a toy.

And is AIDS science or nature? Did it come out of a **petri** dish or a monkey? As far as

I know you can only get HIV from a blood transfusion or sex. And the scientists say it originally came from a monkey of some kind. Now I'm pretty sure we can't do blood transfusions between humans and monkeys. *Do you see where this is going?*

Millions of people have died unnecessarily because they won't legalize prostitution. Okay...I'll explain.

Thirty years ago, there was most likely a scientific nerd with big black glasses who couldn't pick up a woman if his life depended on it. He went to the bar, got loaded and got shot down all night. He went back to his lab, gave one of his monkeys a roofie and...did what he did. The rest is history.

Now if prostitution was legal, he would have had a couple drinks, got his nut and passed out in his Gremlin.

It's so *easy* figuring these 'complex' things out that it scares me.

———

What do we want? Legal prostitution, legal pot and newer, wackier inventions. Stop with the phones already!! We got it!

I think the world is spinning too fast. You know, too many electronic gizmos and thingamabob TV's… (*Okay, plasma TV's, thank you*). Is there really this great demand for speed? Or, is it just ten assholes bugging the V.P. of *Apple*? Then he threatens the foreman's job. So the foreman cracks the whip on the peons that are designing the new phones and computers and they come out with a faster unit than the one they spent a billion dollars on just last month.

"That's it! We're good." Now get those great big brains working on more important stuff. Isn't there a need for space travel and time machines? You're damn right there is! Now get those monkeys working on that. **Speed is not everything**. Look at any zombie movie in the last five years. They run as fast as cheetahs. (*And that sucks cause I can't*). They can even jump over chain link fences. *That was a big part of my defense. Hide behind a chain link fence. Not anymore.*

I just saw a movie where a zombie's arm got chopped off with a machete and the arm chased this idiot around the barn. Now these movies are really getting dumb.

And more is not always better. There was a scene in this one movie where thirty-five people were having an orgy in some cheap motel room and some big zombie kicked down the door and machine gunned the shit out of everybody for two solid minutes. Nothing but smoke and carnage. The next scene was in the motel room next door. "Honey, did you hear that?"

Has the writer of this movie ever *been* to a motel? If you turn the T.V. down a little bit you can hear the bed bugs banging beneath your pillow. There are no walls beneath the crumbling, yellow wallpaper. If you lean against the wall in some of these places, your image will even appear in the next room.

As a traveling performer I end up in a lot of motel rooms every year and they scare the hell out of me. But it's not intruders. Hell, man! I keep a 9mm under my pillow.

Nope, it's the 'local residents' that come out when I turn the lights off. I Lysol the shit out of everything before the lights dim. Two things I don't like about myself are my great hearing and my overactive imagination. I'll be almost out and then I'll hear a noise, "What was that? Was that six legs or eight?"

I played in a honky tonk in the Deep South once and my room was next to the outhouse. When I went inside, my bed was vibrating…but it wasn't a vibrating bed. I went to the general store and picked up moose traps, fly traps, rat traps, roach repellent, industrial strength Lysol – heavy on the lye. Uh…and a shotgun just in case. Then I set a controlled fire a foot away from the bed and hermetically sealed myself in a heavy duty trash bag. Then I drank a bottle of Jack and fell asleep with the light on. Next morning I realized I should've probably just slept in my van. *Duh.*

The technology for getting rid of undesirables may seem like it's dragging, but with everything else, I just sit back and watch.

―――――

Technology is moving so fast it's skipping the natural progression of 'gizmo-ship.' Did any of you have a rotary cell phone? I know I didn't. And except for the guys working on the telephone poles, I've never seen anyone else with one. No, they went straight to push button.

Now they have phones so small you need a toothpick to dial. Why? When does all this stop? Probably when they put that chip in our heads and hear a ringing in our ear. Yup! Progress! Your head is the phone.

*Stop fixing us. We're **not** broken.*

―――――

I think a big market to come up in a couple years will be tattoo removal.

A whole generation is going to wake up and say, "What the fuck was I thinking?" I love my tattoos and I might get another one, but they mean something to me. But I've met people that have gotten tattoos of the latest Disney movie characters.

"You're 32 and you just had the crab from *The Little Mermaid* put on your butt cheek? DUDE!!"

And there's a lot of new technology to help Mother Earth. Everybody is getting 'green.'

But every month it seems like someone says, "We should do *more* for the planet. But what about our kids?"

Have you seen pictures of what the average child's room looks like? We couldn't possibly screw up the planet that badly. If you were thinking of getting a new Hummer and said 'no' because of your kid…you only live once, pal. And secretly your kid doesn't like you anyway. So fuck em!

"But we're putting holes in the ozone layer."

Where? Where do you see holes? I looked at the sky a thousand times and I don't see any holes. If you're looking at those big fluffy white things, those are called clouds. See how they move? Holes don't move. Except you. You're a hole and you move.

And whatever happened to acid rain? Wasn't that supposed to destroy the planet too? There's a paragraph written about it in my kid's history book. And at the time, people were freaked out about acid rain.

"Don't drink it! You can get diarrhea or your kids can have birth defects!"

Really? And where are these two-headed hunchback babies from pregnant women walking in the acid rain?

I like when people talk about something that you know they know nothing about.

"Cockroaches can survive a nuclear war."

How do you know that? Were you at a Hiroshima slum and witnessed this with your own eyes? I had a roach a couple years ago and he couldn't survive a ball-peen hammer to the head. They die too, so shut up!

———

I love technology but I ignore a lot of it. I just don't care about it. But there is one field I think every guy should keep an eye on. And that field is…

Artificial insemination. Fellas, we are almost jobless. Once women discover the pull cord on the lawnmower, we will have only one job left. "Well, you can't make babies without us. You can't replace the pinga!"

Actually they did. Can you see one of those egotistical scientists come out and tell us we're unemployed? I can hear the geek now…

"Well, what we did is replace the man's semi-operational pinga with a small turkey baster. Shoot in a small amount of the donor's baby juice where the pinga used to go and 'Bang!' There it is!"

Me: "But without donors, you're nothing."

Nerd: "Technically."

Me: "So we still have a job?"

Nerd: "Yes, you still have a job…for the moment."

It's just a matter of time before women take over the planet and wipe all us men right out. And if artificial sperm doesn't work out, I see a great job opening coming up in the future.

Okay…it's all women; no men except for a few because the artificial sperm made mutants, and women would still like to assure their survival. They would save a few men to be tied to beds and women would pay an agency (*not you*) to inseminate her while you're tied down. They also keep a Viagra drip in your arm to assure constant satisfaction…to the customer only.

"I would like to fill out an application now and you can keep it on file."

"Are you experienced?"

"Oh yeah, I've done it before. If you'd like to test me, I wouldn't be offended."

That would be a great job although there would be that constant pressure knowing you will be killed when your pinga stops working. I could see my pinga getting tired of it so he reaches over, grabs a scalpel, cuts himself free and jumps out the window.

That would be a day of mourning...

Chapter 3:
Sexless Stories About Animals

So I was over at my aunt's house and she has a parrot; a real "Polly want a cracker" pirate parrot. And he's pretty cool. He only says 'beer pong' and 'boobies,' but that's okay – those are two of my favorite phrases.

I did something really dangerous then; I let my mind function. And this is what it said to me...

Imagine if other pets could talk and what they might say.

A dog would probably be like, "I love you. You're my universe. I love you more now. My bowl's empty. Feed me. I love you more now. Time to lick myself for the 381st time today. How about you? Your crotch, okay? Go grab the peanut butter and we can work out a deal."

A cat...I don't think a cat would surprise anyone with what he'd say. "Hey, come here.

Yeah you, get closer! A little closer! Okay, fuck you. I'll be back in an hour and we can do it again." He couldn't give you the finger because he only has four…so fuck YOU feline!

I don't think I'd care what a pet fish would say even if you *can* hear him through the water. He spends his life swimming from the underwater castle to the filter a thousand times a day. By the time he learns to talk, his mind will be as soft as a fresh loaf of Wonder bread.

I hope a fish is like a stoner with Alzheimer's, otherwise it'd go insane. "Oh, wow! Look…a castle. That's cool. Hey, it's a bubble maker. Wow, look…there's a castle."

A friend of mine has a tarantula. *Why?* I have no damn idea. It's an eight-legged scootch…pre 80's. I couldn't imagine that talking. Maybe it would giggle insanely like Peter Lorre, and plot. It looks tough but its mortal enemy is the bottom of a shoe – so that kind of takes away the horror factor.

And what about horses? I don't know what a female horse would say, but a male horse I think would constantly try to get the male human to invite his wife into the barn for a three-way.

…But that's just me. If I was a horse with this brain I'd have my own reality show: "Who am I Banging Today?" People like watching animals have sex…and don't deny it! There was a people stampede at the zoo when the rhinos were hammering it out. You never saw so many people filming at the zoo. So don't tell me a horse nailing a goat is not a *huge* ratings grabber.

I got a little confused the day I got a dog for my kids. We went to an animal orphanage and let them pick it out. "One dog and you two have to agree." Not an easy task for two kids that used to argue about what flavor air actually is.

But within three minutes they both agreed on a Siberian husky. Why? It had one blue eye and one brown, so it was the coolest.

Well, I found out you have to apply to adopt a pet; they won't just give you an animal. Five pages of paperwork. Now here's the confusing part…

First question: Name? What are we going to name him?

"Jack," says one son.

"Dumbass," says the other.

Okay. Jake the Dumbass.

Address? He's going to live at our house so I put our address.

Schedule? What the hell? I guess he'll wake, I'll let him out to do his thing, feed him and leave the TV on while I'm at work.

Smoking? He smokes? As long as it's not tobacco.

Drinking? He drinks too? Christ, he's me in a scruffy fur coat. How can he afford to smoke and drink?

Then one of the girls walked by so I asked her about some of the questions. "Excuse me, but why is this dog allowed to smoke?"

And she looked at me like I was the dumbest man alive. Looking back on it, I was.

Then the words dripped from her lips like wet cement, "YOU, sir. Do YOU smoke?"

AAHHH…now that made sense.

———

I love pets, but I don't think I could have one now in L.A.

The last time I was in L.A. the thing that stood out for me, in the name of freakiness, was that around almost every corner was a pet masseuse.

Right! A place you can go so that your *pet* can have a massage.

My cat, Norton, does not need a massage. But on a completely unrelated subject, can you flip these people a couple bucks for a 'Happy Ending?" That's something Norton would really like. He would think I was the greatest if I got his 'pigtail' straightened for his birthday.

They also have pet chiropractors to keep their spines straight.

Really? Has my cat been doing a lot of heavy lifting lately? He can't get his fat ass off the sofa without falling, much like half the people I know.

Pet therapists. *Come on.* If you give your pet some attention when you get home, they're generally pretty happy. Does the dog talk to these guys and actually voice his problems? "He leaves me home every day and leaves the TV on. It's always, *The View*. I just want to hang myself with my own leash."

Every dog I know just barks. If you understand what they say, you may need some therapy yourself.

Know what else is coming? Preventive pet medicine. Leading the way is cat proctology. That's where the money is. Sticking a finger in a cat's ass…

How's the visual on that one for you? Coming in nice and clear?

———

Did you ever do something stupid just to see how it would all work itself out in the end? It could have been anything – a triple dose of ex-lax – anything. *Oh, and if you try the ex-lax thing, give yourself a couple days to recuperate.*

Before I had my cat declawed, I let Norton just tear my hand up; he was scratching and chewing on it. I just watched him, fighting the pain, watching myself bleed…but don't worry, it wasn't my bowling hand. Hell No!

Norton tired very quickly. Ten seconds later he'd roll over and start purring. I have a bipolar cat. He's like Jekyll and Hyde but he's so freakin cute. *Is it strange to wonder how vicious your cat will get just by grabbing his tail?*

Then it occurred to me that he spends half his life in his poop box. When he's bored, he digs stuff up and buries it on the other side of his box. I get him catnip but he keeps convincing me to smoke it with him. What can I do? So he plays with his turds. It doesn't concern me…TILL NOW.

I have microscopic feline excretion swimming around in my open wounds. I might want to do something about that. I flew – not ran, but *flew* – into the bathroom. I scrubbed my hand for five minutes with Lye and a steel wool pad…which I found out later was the wrong thing to do. Soap and warm water…*Who knew?*

So I'm in the emergency room and the doctor says to me, "You'd have been better off not doing anything."

Then I got a tetanus shot and some antibiotics. Norton got a trip to the vet.

Guess what's gonna happen if he keeps humping my leg? Norton will be afraid to come near me. He'll be wondering what else I'm going to have chopped off.

I'm not sure where I stand with having male animals fixed like that. I'm not an animal psychiatrist and I don't claim to be, but I think that has to be pretty traumatic for an animal to look down and say, "Hey, what the fuck happened here? They were there before I went to sleep."

That's why a cat meows a lot after…you know…snip snip. He's saying, "I lost my balls. Someone took my balls. Where are my balls?" *(Sounds a lot like a man who's just gotten married)*

I think if you give him a shot of something that keeps his little pinga from getting hard, he'd be a little happier. He can lick himself for a month and it's still a slinky.

One thing Norton and I have agreed upon is that during certain situations we would eat each other. Oh yeah, we made a pact. If I die in bed alone and he runs out of food, he's allowed to eat me. And if we both live through the apocalypse and there isn't *any* food, he's my Saturday night chili.

It's all in my will.

————

I've had cats and I've had dogs; I don't label myself. They both eat, poop and they both found my stash and ate it. And I knew they ate it even before I knew it was gone. When I got home I got a different kind of reception. I opened the door and found the dog lying on his back, passed out with *Cheetos* dust all around his muzzle. And he was watching Jerry Springer. What an asshole!!! *No, not my dog.* I had no idea what was up until I found a chewed-up, drool-covered baggie. I put it all together after that.

A couple years later he died. So then I got a cat. It hurt when my dog died so I decided to get a cat. If he died, fuck it…he's a cat. But I've had Norton for a few years now and I'm getting attached to him.

One day I came home and heard the TV. As I walked closer, I heard, "Okay, Tawanda, the nine DNA tests are in. Would you like to know who the father of your unborn child is?"

I could actually hear my mind working…click… click… click… "MY POT!" As I ran into my bedroom, I stepped on the chewed up little baggie. *DAMMIT.*

I might have mentioned a couple hundred times how pot is a great aphrodisiac…cause it is.

Well, it must work for cats the same way. I sat down next to him, cleaned off his *Cheetos* dust and went to pet him. One stroke down his back and he let out a purr so loud, it scared me. Like petting a hornet's nest…very unnerving. And he just wouldn't keep his ass out of my face. I have no idea what that was about.

If you ever had a dog and a cat, you know they are very different.

A dog is under your feet from the time you come into the house till the time you leave. *Very* needy. Whereas a cat, you might not see for a month. The only clue that it still lives there is when you come home and the food bowl's empty and the litter box is full or that day you cross paths in the hallway.

"Hey."

"Sup."

———

If my dog has an accident at night, I'll step in it. That WILL be my first step of the day. I go from warm bed to lukewarm puppy poopy. Judging from its warmth and texture, if I would have gotten up twenty minutes sooner he might have made it outside.

Now my cat, Norton, he'll poop by my bed for spite. He's a bastard. And when you pick him up after you step on his turds and look him in the eyes and say, "Why the fuck did you do that?" You get that 'look' that says, "Hey, the box was all the way over there. Why did you step on that anyway? I just wanted you to pick it up. That's how I get my jollies…moron!"

I think we give cats a little too much credit for brains because they always look so serious. Cats are too 'cool' to show emotion so we think they're smarter. A dog wears its heart on its slobbering two-foot tongue. If a dog is happy, he's all over you. If it did something wrong, it will hide or mope.

A cat? Nothing. The only time I ever saw Norton show true emotion was last summer. I was fooling around with my sons' water pistol when Norton came around the corner and I got him…right on the nose. Now, you *know* I don't like it when animals curse. Cursing is for us – the ones at the top of the food chain. But the look he gave me said, "What the fuck was that?"

Then he ran across the backyard faster than I ever saw a cat move. I don't know what crazy world Norton thinks he's King of, but this shocked him back to reality...for a bit.

Wait...we were talking about animal poop...

So last summer I was walking around in a field in sneakers with no socks. I got a stone in one sneaker so I took it off and put my foot right down in a pile of rabbit pellets. ...I put my weight on it too. There was a pile of icky jelly beans stuck to my foot between my toes and under one nail. I WAS SO DISGUSTED!

It was a *pile*. That rabbit must have been sick, or it was its own little cesspool or something.

Somebody told me it might have been deer poop. I was like, "Really? A big animal like that craps jelly beans?" Must feel like anal beads coming out; I'm surprised deer don't giggle when they poop.

Deer: "I have to hold it a little…longer…CRAP! (poop poop poop – HaHaHaHaHaHa.)

Hunter: "Okay, deer. Don't move."

Deer: "Come on, man. I *had* to go. You didn't even see me until I laughed. Is that the headline you want? Man shoots pooping deer? Oh, yeah…that would look *great* on the cover of *Field & Stream*! Dumbass."

Chapter 4:
A Reality Show About a Reality Show

The most powerful people in the world **aren't** presidents and kings…they are weathermen. Oh, yeah…those guys just mention blizzards and an entire city will squeeze themselves into an Acme in about twenty minutes. And it's always for milk and bread. Like you can live on French toast for a week? Only if your milk holds out. And if it 'turns' during the week, you have to wait till it transforms into low grade cheese before you can eat it.

That's why I'd get a skid of water…lasts for years. So while your dead carcass is hugging that bad milk/good cheese, I can walk in, grab it…AND your bread, and wait out the storm. I'll be eating grilled cheese sandwiches while the other survivors will be dining on rats and pigeons.

See? It's important to think these things through.

Another thing about 'weather people' is that they don't **have** to be right, but who can say when they're wrong?

"Today is going to be partly sunny and tomorrow is going to be partly cloudy."

Really? Is that what the coin flip told you? You have a billion dollar Doppler satellite and that's the best you have? I may as well call a friend who lives 100 miles west of me.

"Good morning, Phil. Say…what's the weather like there? Uh huh. So nice you'd go to the beach if you had one? Thanks, Phil. Yeah, I'm going to the beach."

I've fallen in lust with more weather girls than any other profession. And the worst news she can give me is that it's going to rain this weekend. That's why I bought a house across the street from a liquor store. The party never stops.

But look at the rest of the news people. The anchors are going to tell you about fires, murders and hideous happenings across the globe.

And the sports guy *(sorry ladies, they're always dudes),* and I don't swing that way no matter *how* nice his voice is, says, "And the Eagles kicked the…"

Yeah, I know. I watched it. All fans are gonna watch the game. If they don't watch the game then they don't care who won.

I'd love to change the news a little bit. You know…just tweak it.

…A half hour of the weather girl in a fantasy costume telling us about weather around the world…"And tomorrow, the Sahara desert is expecting a monsoon."

Yeah. Keep flipping that coin, baby.

———

Have you noticed how the news is now trying to make the bad news sound just a little better by giving you a fact about the story you really don't need?

"And he was shot by no less than seventeen bullets. That's the 53rd murder this year so far, but we're down two murders from this time last year. Not bad, right?"

"A twin-engine Cessna crashed today killing the pilot, co-pilot and all six passengers. Apparently, it ran out of fuel. However, it crashed into a landfill. I mean, how lucky was that? Maybe he knew he was doomed and aimed for it. How considerate. It might suck for the ambulance folks but at least we won't blow a lot of cash getting rid of the wreckage."

"And for all you guys that like it 20-below and windy? You will absolutely love tomorrow and the rest of the week. But, be careful if you have to go outside."

You know what I think when I hear that? "Fuck this town! I'm moving closer to the equator. I do not want to live in a town where the weather can literally kill you. I mean, I do have people that don't really like me, but I really don't want to be killed by my environment. I never want to think about the fact that if I miss a weather report it could kill me. Where's my freakin luggage? And there's always somebody standing there saying:

'Hey, someone has to live there.'

"Oh yeah? Well, fuck you. You live there and I'll drop by and chip you out during the spring thaw. Then I'm gonna laugh my ass off over your frozen carcass."

How would you like to freeze to death and have the whole town talk about it for the next eighty years? "Hey, remember that dude that forgot his scarf and his aorta froze?"

"Yeah, and when he fell over his head snapped off his body. That was so cool."

That is **not** going to be me. I know how I want to die and it's not by the freakin weather. HOW? Uh, okay. I want to be having an incredibly filthy dream and just as I reach the ultimate moment of my existence, every atom in my entire being just goes in the opposite direction. In a nanosecond my body would not exist. So I'd be either a spirit or…not.

You guys believe in spirits and the soul and all that crap, right? Yeah, me too. I think of all that stuff in the movie, "Men in Black." There's like a little alien creature in our heads that drive our bodies like big machines.

"Orion's…ba…ba…belt." I really liked that little alien. But getting back to TV, it just keeps getting worse. It's so bad I was offered a TV show a few years back and I turned it down.

———

They should have a reality show that's *actually* real. Here's an idea, call it "Housewife."

Lady: "Hi, I'm Jane. First, I'm going to start the dishwasher. My husband and I hate eating off dirty dishes.

"Now I'm going to put the sheets in the washer. Jeff has been coming home quite amorous lately so the sheets smell a bit funky. It probably has something to do with the new office girl they hired. My husband may think I'm a dope…but I'm not." (*red eyes flare into the camera*)

"Now I'm on my way to the doctor's office. I think I have a urinary tract infection from all the extra *inadequate* sex we've been having. I may put antifreeze in his coffee tomorrow. You'll just have to tune in to see." (*flash big white smile*)

———

I think I've developed a solution to raise money for this country.

A lot of states are poor…*real* poor. If your state needs money, talk your statesmen into having "PayPerView" public executions. **I'd** pay forty bucks for that.

Friday night, you invite some friends over. They each chip in $5 and bring some beer. It's a party. And before the main event, you get the exciting back-story:

Announcer: "Bobby killed the Henderson family after Bill Henderson cut

Bobby off as he came from Wawa. So Bobby followed them home and burned down their house as they slept. And HEEERRRE'S Bobby!"

"Bobby, is there anything you'd like to say to the millions of people spitting at their flat screen TV's at home?"

Bobby: "Uh…I hope I don't shit my pants."

Announcer: "We all do Bobby. Good Luck in Hell, Scumbag."

And if it starts getting too technical and slow, bring out a couple of clowns with bottles of seltzer to keep the laughs rolling.

Fuck the future deceased; he's gonna be beef jerky in a couple minutes anyway. Sorry if I'm a little low on sympathy.

Death like that is fine but I don't like when people say fans of racecar driving are only interested in watching accidents. That is SO not true. They have good corn dogs at the track too.

But that's a horrible thing to say. What if people apply that way of thinking to other things?

"People go to zoos hoping a tiger will leap over a wall and eat some children."

"People go to hotdog eating contests to see if someone chokes."

"People watch reality TV because…because…hell if I know. Maybe one of their friends is on it."

One thing I know about reality TV is if an ex-girlfriend invites me to a Jerry Springer show, I tell her I'm busy. If it wasn't for DNA testing, Jerry would still be mayor of Chicago.

This is every episode: "Tonya just wants to know who the father of her baby is. Let's bring out the 157 guys she fucked and test them."

Know what I *really* dislike about TV these days? You don't graduate to anything else. Most shows are 'flash in the pans.'

"Okay, here's your million. Now go!"

No advancing to anything. I'll tell you who moved up! Gavin McLeod. He started out as a lowly sailor on "McHale's Navy." *Seamen, Duh.* He got out of the service for a while and became Mary Tyler Moore's office buddy. **That** was nice.

Then he must have missed the ocean because he became captain of "The Love Boat." You see? The gigs just got better for Gavin because of his talent and hard work. Even Ernest Borgnine and Tim Conway moved up. They went on to become retired superheroes on "SpongeBob SquarePants." *You don't get better than that.* Well…maybe a singer on "Glee."

Okay, how many of you think it's disturbing that I know that? Yeah, I have a head full of useless information. I don't know who the Speaker of the House is, or the price of gold, but I **can** repeat every line to the "Speed Racer" episode: "The Mach 5 vs. the Mammoth Car."

I should probably be more in touch with politics but I have enough aggravation in my life right now. They're gonna do what they're gonna do anyway, so fuck em!

If this country gets in too bad of shape, I'll throw a door in the ocean and go to Cuba. "How do you like that, communist bi-otch?"

But…back to reality TV shows. Most of those people will be forgotten by my next bowel movement.

I'm pitching my own reality TV show called, "Trailer Trash Wars." It's kind of like "Cops," but without the cops. I lived in one for seven years. *In a trailer park, not with the cops*. Friends are friends in the park, and everybody else can chupa your Marlboro-smoking pinga. But if you can't stomach hard living, Friday night was the worst. Everybody drinking and fighting. One old man bitching about dog turds on his speck of grass. Just standing in his underwear, bitching.

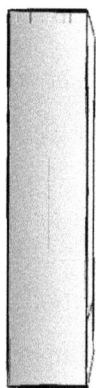
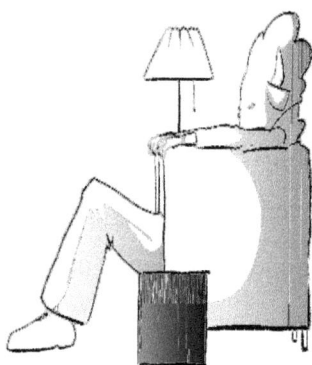

And the heavyset female owner of the dog, who's obviously not wearing underwear, standing and demanding he get the turd DNA tested to prove it's her dog.

Then there was Jerry. He lost his license for ten years, so he sits on his Harley revving the engine, imagining he's blowing down the highway.

One little 'trailer park mystery' seemed to take forever to solve. *But sometimes I'm a little slow in the head.*

At three o'clock in the afternoon I'm looking out my window for no reason whatsoever, and I see 'Mr. Smith' sneakin out of 'Mrs. Johnson's.' He wasn't walkin out, he was sneakin out.

And I'm thinking to myself, "Now what's he doing over there? He knows Mr. Johnson's still at work...DING."

"Oh my god, I just witnessed an affair."

"What else is going on here?"

Apparently, I never noticed A LOT. One guy would shake hands with a hundred people a day. I found out that in that handshake he was passing dope. *Very* exciting.

And a fat senior citizen was a prostitute. I couldn't believe it. She was hideous. I wouldn't bang her to save my life and here there were…guys paying her for sex. If she hadn't left her shade up that one time, I'd never have believed it. I think it shocked my pinga; for a week it wouldn't work. As a matter of fact, the dealer was always over there. Wonder what was up with that?

I lived there in my redneck years. There was nothing city-like about this trailer park…except the 93 Spanish folks living in the trailer down the block. I was never in their trailer but I imagined it was nothing but beds.

In the words of the immortal Art Carney: "Strange and wondrous."

———

I think it's funny how the only time you hear a southern accent on TV is with these two shows:

"Swamp Wars," which is a bunch of good ole' boys hunting gators in a swamp. You can't get a more southern job than that. I put on the subtitles just so I know what they're talking about. They sound like that cartoon character 'Paw Rug' on the "Hillbilly Bears." *Dbadadelieo da rucka rucka...gator turds, hehhehheh.*

The other show is "Jerry Springer." Yeah, let's pick on Springer tonight. No, don't go 'Whoo, Whoo' here. Don't you think if someone invites you to "Springer," that before you accept you may want to re-examine the last 6 to 9 months of your life to see if you're **on** the show and not **at** the show?

"Let's see…thinking back I got my wife's sister pregnant, my meth lab blew up in the church's basement, and I'm practicing the art of trans-species love making…" *I'm good, let's go.*

Half the time that's what it is…a guy cheating on his girl, his guy, his cattle, or his favorite shrub.

The other episodes focus on some hideous broad that's gonna have the east wing of Rahway Penitentiary DNA tested. And it's always the guard who 'done it.' Half the time I'm amazed she's not a virgin. How can you stay aroused looking at THAT? And don't tell me, 'it's not looks, it's personality."

She had sex with fourteen guys in six hours, so I'm not digging her personality much either. What else you got? That is a crazy talent though. I couldn't make love to fourteen women in six hours. I'd probably be the only one walking away from that deal with a smile…and a lot of women would be saying, "What the hell was that?"

I'm more of a 'quality not quantity' type of guy. And really, I see me stroking out because of too much Viagra by around girl #8.

———

I think shows like "CSI" are desensitizing us. Two actors speaking their lines, sucking back some coffee over the open chest plate of the victim of a cabbie hit and run:

Actor 1: "My contract's up this year. I'm going for double. Say…this is a cute victim. Is she still warm?"

Actor 2: "I don't think you really want to do that. It's pretty bad."

Actor 1: "Oh my God is, is that…"

Actor 2: "It used to be."

Actor 1: "I'm scarred, I tell you…scarred for life."

Actor 2: "Think how she feels. But wait, here's her dead girlfriend. Look at her…"

Actor 1: "WOOWW, that's much better."

I bet if one of us walks down the street later and walks by a dead body, the most that victim would get is, "HUH."

I know your average New Yorker has probably had to deal with *this* a few times:

N.Y. Guy 1: "Hey Mario, look. Another dead guy."

N.Y. Guy 2: "No. Pete, it's the same guy. See? The piano wire is still wrapped around his neck."

N.Y. Guy 1: "Oh yeah…Fug'em, his problems are over. Now me…"

N.Y. Guy 2: "Fogetaboutit, Pete."

I was into the "CSI" shows for a couple years but they started getting silly. There's David Caruso standing in an interrogation room, waving an evidence bag at some chump sitting there with his hands folded.

Perp: "You have nothing on me so let me go."

Caruso: "Yes we do. We found an eyelash at the crime scene."

Perp: "Man, that can be anybody's eyelash."

Caruso: "Yes, but this eyelash has your fingerprints and semen on it."

Okay, I'm done.

I would really like TV to stop making references to semen. My God, what is wrong with people who want to hear about that? On the show "Survivor" they *live* off that stuff. That is white gold to the writers of that show:

> Host: "So, Bill, you can win 10 points for your team if you eat this concoction of

coconut, sea bass and a secret ingredient. And this week's secret ingredient is…animal semen!"

> *Harold and Kumar again, dude.*

———

I think all this started with "All in the Family." Someone would knock on the front door and Edith would answer:

> "Mrs. Bunker, I'd like to talk to your husband." Toilet flushes…

> Edith: "He'll be down in just a minute."

Up until then nobody went to the bathroom on TV. They held it in. It was in their contracts. Now they slather baby batter around like whipped cream at a birthday party.

In a couple years, they'll be talking about semen on "Sesame Street."

Bert: "Ernie, what are you putting on your cracker?"

Ernie: "You really don't want to know, Bert."

Chapter 5:
Here's the Sex Stuff You Were Looking For

There is a solution for every sexual fetish on your computer. One day go deep into the sick part of your psyche (*everybody owns one*), come up with any sexual scenario and look it up on the computer.

Say you want to see couples peeing on each other…it's there. You want to see a bunch of beagles lick peanut butter off a woman who is completely covered with it…it's there.

I got sucked up in the bait. You know what that is…right? It's when there's a video you can see that says: "Disturbing." Well, I **had** to look at that. Could be anything. Could be a girl squatting on an orange highway cone…who knows?

But it wasn't. There was a guy with an ax in his hand and his pinga on the table. I clicked off immediately. No thank you.

And it's all on your computer. But before computer porn you had TV and video porn. And, I guess before that, they had radio porn. Somewhere between "Fibber McGee" and "Our Miss Brooks" you had "Prohibition and the Pinga:"

Announcer: "When we last saw John and Mary, Mary had been shot in the stomach during a botched speakeasy robbery and John carried Mary to Dr. McGillicutty's basement clinic."

John: "Doctor, will Mary be alright?"

Dr. M.: "Yes John. I got the slug out. Now she needs her rest." (*Ring, Ring*) "Oh, that's my phone, please excuse me."

Mary: "John...is that you?"

John: "Yes Mary...I'm here."

Mary: "John...come...closer."

John: "Yes Mary."

(*Unzip...sounds: slurp, slurp, slurp, gulp, gulp, gulp*)

John: "Gee Mary, thank you. That was swell."

Mary: (*cough*) "You're welcome." (*cough, cough*).

I don't want to star in porn, and I'm pretty sure I don't want to direct porn, but I can write porn. Depending on the strength of the coffee, I can bang out (*excuse the pun*) between six and eight porn movies an hour. What takes time is coming up with titles; that could take up to another minute. Here's an example: A cable installer rings a doorbell and a beautiful blonde in a bathrobe opens the door.

Guy: "Hello, I'm here to install your cable."

Lady: "You're a little late."

Guy: "I'm very sorry, ma'am."

Lady: "Well, actually, you're right on time."

Okay, cue music. I want music that sounds like this…"DADADaDaDa bink DADAdadada benk DADADAdada bank." (Yeah, we compose the music too but we get a whole ten minutes to write an entire porno. It's not that tough to write this shit, believe me.)

I couldn't come up with a title for this one so out of frustration I called it, "The Cable Pinga." After that I started my own franchise. We had "The Plumber Pinga," "The Mailman Pinga," and "Pizza Party Pinga." That one was more of a gangbang. They're worth more money so I try to write a couple of G.B.'s a day. That's porn writers 'speak.'

And most are filmed in the summer. If I'm gonna pick a favorite season, I'll go with summer. A quick visit to the beach will tell you why. Chicks in bathing suits. Nothing builds testosterone faster.

And it's so easy to incorporate the summer holidays into the bedroom. Memorial Day...you just wheel the grill into the bedroom. When the time is right just pull out and flip the steaks, than continue he'ing and she'ing.

4th of July...you can have bottle rockets shoot out of the headboard as you both, you know, squirt squirt.

And, yes, I don't like the word 'orgasm.' My god! For the greatest ten seconds of a person's life you'd have thought they would have come up with a better word than that.

"GushGush." There, that's a better word.

And Labor Day…the end of summer…you can have a three-way with a keg of beer. You know, I might just do that this weekend. Some of my best weekends included a woman and a keg…

Halloween speaks for itself. Crazy sex fantasies there. I might come (or, cum) as the Easter Bunny. I'll get one with real fur and then turn it inside out. How about a rabbit costume made out of mink? I'll have P.E.T.A. worshippers shooting me with paintballs from every angle. Please, not the cookies…

It's funny, animals love me and animal activists hate me.

But I had a goal. I wanted to be the first to get laid on the moon. Then your life would be on reality TV until your three weeks dead. Well, they have to put you on one final tour. And if they filmed the first sex on the moon, you and your pinga would be signing autographs for years. The same way everybody wanted to shake Neil Armstrong's hand when he got back, everyone is going to want to shake your...uh...well, you know.

And **that** could be a lot of fun.

Again, I'd like to volunteer for this mission. Here is my sexual resume. Please disregard the first couple years...I have no excuses; I was just nervous.

I'm always volunteering for these dangerous missions. I must be some kind of hero wannabe. Give me a million dollars and a cause and I'm there. And I'll do my **best** not to fuck it up.

———

Sex in space is one thing, sex in jail is another. Most people probably don't like it. You have to be tough in prison. "Yeah, I stabbed that guy for looking at me twice."

Look, you can't be in jail with really big, angry guys because you had parking tickets. I would have been bitchified; it'd be 'shit on a shingle' time...that's breakfast for all you non-cons.

The only guy I remember is Bruno. *Can't forget a guy's name when it's tattooed across his forehead; it makes a lasting impression.*

So as I'm leaving prison, Bruno says to me, "Hey Buff, I'll call you when I get out. We'll go have a few beers and bust some fuckin' heads."

I changed my number seventeen times since I got out...just in case.

———

Do you guys believe in ghosts? You know...beings that live ghost lives...eating ghost food...having ghost sex.

Maybe we're a ghost world to *them*. Maybe sometimes we appear to them and we don't know it. All of a sudden, whatever it is you're doing is seen by people on the other side. So watch your nose picking and masturbation events. You don't want to have a fuzzy picture of yourself fiddling your faddle in their ghost "National Enquirer." There's a headline you don't want: "Ghostly figure pulling his ripcord. Picture on page 28."

You'll be *really* popular at the ghost Acme checkout line.

There are some who want you to believe there are ghosts that come to your bed…for sex. An incubus and a succubus. Hell if I know which is which, but that can be a problem. Suppose a gay ghost shows and you don't swing that way. If you don't want to be crappin ectoplasm for a week, you might want to learn to sleep on your back.

If there is a ghost world and I could slide in and out of it, I'd do the same thing to them that they do to me…hide their keys.

Could you imagine having sex with someone on the other side? Then you just pop back to this world? How badass would that be! Like Romeo and Juliet on acid. Ladies and gentlemen, think of the benefits of that. But you may want to hit up Wal-Mart for some rubber sheets.

My real fantasy is sex in a mink-tailored rabbit suit.

And not to sound insulting to 'large' ladies, cause Lord knows I rolled around with a few, but there is not a reason in the world to make quadruple extra-large *Wonder Woman* costumes. Please stop trying to destroy my illusion. I **love** Lynda Carter.

Ladies, let me tell you a little bit about your man. He will stick it anywhere he can.

If an alien…you know, from space (*duh*) landed on Earth and through some sort of 'thought trading' told us she was a female and was like a cute blob of space blubber with a bunch of holes that look like… holes, your average man will be on it within seconds. To be the first man to have sex with a beautiful space alien blob, you'd probably burn out your zipper pulling it down.

And there will be no protection at all. We all would try something new…once. El Natural. You'll have to film that. Yeah, Space Alien Porn…better known as SAP flicks. There'd be 10, 20…30 guys at the same time, banging some fat, ugly alien bitch from another universe. *There's a billion dollar idea just in 3D DVD sales alone!*

———

Oh, by the way…if you're a young child and you found me under your dad's underwear in the top drawer, forget everything you read for the last 49 pages. Now put me back and get the hell out of here! The last thing a child needs to hear are stories about how their dad is basically a sex pervert willing to pay money to watch SAP movies.

Oh…and SAP movies aren't called that because they're porn. It's because what the guys are banging is the alien's nostrils. When she takes a deep breath, all the pingas pull the men into the alien, and all that's left is little piles of sap...

———

Do you want to know something about the male animal you may **not** know? Sometime, in the next couple of weeks when you have to 'do it yourself,' 1 in 3 males will use an alien as his...muse. But a shapelier blob made of silicone, with a Kung Fu grip...**that's** the alien for me.

I'm willing to bet a lot of you never really thought of having sex with an alien. But if you caught my last show I talked about three guys having sex with the same watermelon, so banging an alien isn't too much of a stretch.

I give the people what they want. Apparently, a lot of people love hearing about wild, sexual things. And the watermelon story was true...*Yuck*. Do you think they all screwed it at the same time, or they each took turns with it in the bedroom?

Dave: "Come on, Jim. Hurry up. I have to pick my kid up at soccer practice in half an hour."

Jim: "Dude! Do you know how hard it is to get hard over fruit? Very…it's *very* hard, Dave."

I think we covered a lot of sexual ground tonight. There are probably a few things I forgot to cover…like whether or not you can step into a parallel universe where you are your **own** sexual partner and you **have** to do it because you know just what **you** want…sexually.

And in this day and age, it would go just perfect with the times. I know I've had a few people tell me to go fuck myself. Now I can just say…"Okey doke."

Upon further thought, the idea repulses me.

…Let's move on.

———

Okay, here's another sick thought. Think of somebody you'd want to have sex with from the past that's been dead at least a hundred years. And, why? My game, so I go first…Mona Lisa.

She's kinda cute and Italian women just seem to love me.

I could have made the game harder. I could have said name a space alien that looks like me that's been dead for at least a hundred years…

I have GOT to stop drinking during the show. I think my brain cells are countable.

There was one suggestion of making an all-male porn film about the Greeks and calling it, "Trojan Train." And with a Greek soundtrack – which is usually more upbeat – you're bound to see something you've never seen before. Lots o' Passion!

Do you guys mind if I backtrack just a bit? I wanna see what subjects we covered since you got me sidetracked here. I want to see how this line of thought got started and where it went.

Okay…it ended with an all-male Greek porn called, "Trojan Train." Then me banging Mona Lisa. Geez, that sounds pretty bad right there.

Ahh, sex with female self…

―――

I'm willing to bet that half of my fans are psychiatrists. The psychotic American standard: Three men and a melon.

S.A.P. flicks (still *YUCK*)! Sex in jail, sex on the moon and sex on the holidays. Not bad.

And, of course, the least useful but still fun sport of "Blackout Drunken Sex." That's about the only one I can really see women doing.

Some of my favorite women are blackout drunks. They love me but they don't know why. Well…produce sex…come to think of it fruits and vegetables are very possible for a female. I remember this time in Tijuana…

…I'll come back to that.

3-D is something I can see chicks digging. Women were *made* for 3-D. After everything I said, I'd like to make a final statement to bring peace to the world and perhaps be used on my next million seller bumper sticker: "Keep it Human." There's a lot of powerful sexual energy being wasted on dolls and fruit.

I think part of the problem is the cure for horniness is at the tips of our fingers. We're so hooked on sex that we'll stick it anywhere...or in anything.

Do you know what has the right idea? Salmon! They have a fish orgy where they all roll around on each other then swim upstream to die. They know life is not going to get any better. And they don't have to worry about raising the kids...It's perfect.

———

Last weekend was a wild drinking sex party. That was the night I passed out in the hotel fountain… Wasn't even my hotel. Hell if I know how I got there.

I don't know how it started but there was at least seventy people just spread out drinking and having sex. Before I blacked out, this party was huge. That may have been the greatest night of my life and I forgot the whole fuckin thing.

I'm not endorsing this type of lifestyle, but there *is* one thing I like about it and that's the 'pocket treasure hunt' in the morning. You start rummaging through your pockets to find clues to the night before. You might have a million dollars in your wallet…but it's usually more like a buck. And that buck is usually wedged between a couple ATM receipts. If you don't remember *them*, that could be a problem.

"Let's check the date on them. Last night at 10:35, and this morning…3:55. I am so screwed."

So I'm trying to figure out what I bought that late at night. Just about everything is closed. In fact, at that hour you can only buy debauchery. Did you know debauchery comes in tiny little Ziploc bags? No wonder I had so many friends last night; I was sprinkling everybody with magic dust.

So I'm trying to calm myself down. "Don't worry about it. It's only the mortgage."

"FFFUUUCCCKKK!!!!!!!!!!!"

So far, it's looking pretty bad. Until I got to my last pocket. There I found a sheet of paper all crumpled up. So I unfold it and on the top it reads, "Things to use in new sex material segment." **This** is what you folks want to hear.

Sex with more kinds of animals, including a crazy story about insect sex. *What?* Like what? People letting fire ants pierce their genitals, or big bugs? That'd be hard fighting through twenty sets of legs to…*Yuck*. Now **that** would be creepy. The only thing worse than having sex with a bug is a guy waiting to watch a DVD of a guy having sex with a bug.

Yeah, people LOVE porn.

I'm sure if you care to look there are videos of beautiful girls punching guys in the cookies until they pass out. And there are people that would want to watch it too.

You wouldn't believe what these people wanted me to talk about...like masquerade orgies. I've hosted orgies, but never really thought of a theme or masks. Naked people with masks just don't do it for me. Unless just about everyone is ugly, then why bother with an orgy? Crack your own whip then move on with your day. *I wish I was a little more depraved but I'm not.*

Do you have any idea what is on the internet? I saw a six-foot, 700 pound woman let a half dozen 'short people' or 'midgets,' or whatever is politically correct to call them now, do things to her. They were just crawling all over her and jabbing at anything that jiggled with their little pingas. *Once I stopped laughing, I was pretty disgusted.*

Some sick bastard wrote that he wanted to see twins – a brother and sister having sex. And he wrote that he understands they won't be identical twins but they have to look a lot alike. *Duh.* Really? A twin fetish? At what point in your life did that little seed sprout into your subconscious? And how long till it grew into a thought?

One guy wrote something I don't think he thought all the way through. He asked, "Why is there no 3-D porn?"

Well, first off, half the flick is a guy's hairy ass flying towards your face. And second, you all know how these movies end, right? You've seen porn, right? *Liar.*

Well, when the guy reaches the ultimate moment of his existence – you know, squirt squirt – I don't want to see if flying at me.

And stop saying you don't watch porn; you're making me feel self-conscious.

I'm merely a fan of the arts. The one request I really liked was holiday-based porn. I think Christmas is the time you'd reach your widest audience. You'd have three different kinds of movies: Santa banging Mrs. Claus, Santa banging an elf, and Santa lost in the wilderness so he bangs a reindeer. That's a big umbrella there.

Arbor Day porn can be confusing. Is that sex in a tree, under a tree, or with a tree?

I'm just gonna bypass Groundhog Day because there's no way that can end well.

St. Patty's Day will be just a drunken orgy of strangers. So how many of you have woken up naked next to a complete stranger? **There you go**…a few of you have. Luckily for me, it was always with reasonably cute girls.

Do you know the great thing about being a blackout drunk in this position? If you can finagle morning sex, it's like having sex for the first time with her again. Oh, and it cures hangovers. I figured that one out.

———

I'm willing to bet half my pay tonight that at least half of this audience has gone to a zoo, or a farm that was a normal visit. Then…you turned a corner and there was like…two zebras having wild zebra sex. The neck biting and the 'lay that pipe hard' attitude commenced and you stood there and…watched! Maybe it wasn't zebras but…I don't know…two iguanas. Who cares? That's not the point. You watched and wondered: "Did we ever try it like that before?"

I'll bet half of you did and I've got the cash to back it up. Sex happens a lot in zoos. One summer I camped out at the zoo. I was making animal porn. I know there are enough sick fellas out there that will make me rich. I thought I'd start a real trend in movies with "Animal Porn." If you don't like Larry Flynt, you'd really hate me.

I was paying off cotton candy guys and lemonade girls every time they saw anything that looked like 'it' was about to happen. I was going to be rich!

Hey…do you know it's against the law to sell animal porn? Who'd have thought?

———

Some animals like it rough; the Praying Mantis, for example. After sex, the giant female turns around and eats the smaller male mantis…and not in a good way. If I knew that was how it ended, I'd go bang a water bug. I'm sure I could beat up a water bug.

Do you think a female praying mantis is mean and domineering with her husband when they're out in bug society?

Female: "Hurry up, stupid. You're making us late for the Henderson's party."

Male: "I don't want to go to the Henderson's."

Female: "Don't make me eat you. Now get dressed."

Male: "Yes, dear."

The one animal that made me laugh was the gorilla. They're big and tough, right? We learned about gorillas in school. They can rip your arms off your body and bat your head a country mile. And they have a three inch pinga! Oh. Man…where you going with that? No wonder female gorillas always look so pissed. You almost want to flash her – show her what a real primate looks like. She'd probably bend the bars trying to get to you.

You know, I'll bet there are people out there that like flashing animals. Which brings up a question: Do you think a guy was ever flashing an animal and a hawk swooped down and grabbed his junk? I think sometime, somewhere in history, it probably happened.

Ever since man discovered that the pinga has more uses than just urination and procreation, it's been one big, freakin party. "Now, where do I wanna stick it?"

Ever since I heard the story of the three guys banging a watermelon so that one guy could give it to his ex-wife, nothing surprises me! A dude losing his pinga to a hawk while flashing a goat? Yeah, I can see that.

The thing about sex isn't the five seconds of funny noises and squealing, it's the relaxation afterwards. Man...I sleep like a baby after sex. But when I don't have it for a couple weeks, look out! I get mean. That's why I hate election years. I have to abstain from sex for a week or I won't vote. If I don't have sex, I can't wait to get in that booth.

"Okay, which one of you assholes is gonna legalize pot and bring back corporal punishment?" You *have* to have your priorities in order.

Isn't it amazing that you can talk about anything, even animal sex, and it always comes back to the government? That'd be interesting watching an elephant have sex with a donkey.

I'll bet the donkey squeals first.

———

My introduction to the 'double standard' of the world began with *National Geographic*.

In the old editions of *National Geographic*, you'd see pictures of African women with ten-gallon urns of water balanced on their heads as they walked five miles back to the village. There wasn't a fat chick in the bunch. These ladies were tone and had pert boobies. No neck…but **pert** boobies.

And when the women got older, they'd hand down the tradition to their daughters. Then the older women would sit in their huts and knit a blanket until they ballooned up to 400 pounds and died of…fat. And their not-so-pert boobies were bared on the pages. They scared me…and I almost cried. But the pert boobies made me smile. So…my parents canceled my subscription.

I was nine and I liked it; naked women walking around like that was normal. I wanted that fashion and work ethic to be grasped by America. It's a great deal for guys but not for the girls. Even if the guys are naked too.

I think most women would do something about it. Jenny Craig would be a trillionaire and *Curves* would be its own religion.

Most guys who aren't in shape probably don't give a damn. We got what we want.

Do you think it would stop being surreal after about a year? I think almost immediately guys would storm Congress begging them to repeal the public masturbation law.

And it would provide a lot of jobs. Like in a big city, they'd put big spittoons on every street corner. Well, someone has to build these spittoons, deliver these spittoons and empty these spittoons. That's a job that you don't cheap out on with the gloves. You'd probably want the very best. End result? More jobs for glove makers.

See? I'm good at building jobs. And all it took was letting everybody walk around naked and repealing the public masturbation law. Now if a simple country boy like me can think of ways to get the good, old U.S. of A. back to work, why can't our government?

That first time you ventured out into public naked would be the toughest. Most people would probably start off at night…get the feel of it for a while. Every time you pass someone, you'd cover your 'good parts' with your hands.

I think I'd need a few drinks before I set forth on my first walkabout. And it better not be cold or I'm not going!

I think the first conversations with friends and family would be difficult, too:

You: "So that's the famous…"

Me: "Yeah, that's it. And that's your…"

You: "Uh huh. Did the Phillies play today?"

I don't think the public masturbation thing will take off until a big celebrity like Brad Pitt is filmed choking it to a waitress.

I can see the commercial now… "If it's good enough for Brad…"

Here's another moneymaker. If you miss the spittoon you can be fined $25 dollars. More money to help our government.

Vote me mayor, people.

Public masturbation would only be a fad…for a century or two.

Oh…wait…first problem. Where would guys keep their wallets? And keys…and a comb? We can only wedge just so much stuff between our butt cheeks.

And suntan lotion – that could be REALLY important. I don't need my pinga cooked! And we would need to rub the lotion in evenly. You don't want people thinking you missed the spittoon.

I doubt *anybody* would get married then.

———

I love sex but not marriage. Am I weird? I think a marriage license should come with an expiration date. Say…five years with the option to renew. It would save a lot of hard feelings.

"Baby, do you want to do another five years? No? Neither do I."

It's hard to focus on love these days. You walk through the mall and you can fall in love six times before you even hit the food court. No, wait…that's lust.

Did you ever notice that lust and slut have the same letters, and love spelled backwards is evol?

We're all sluts, men and women. If you've had more than ten lovers, you're considered a slut. Even if you do it to yourself you're a slut. *Hey, you're thinking of someone…**slut**.*

Did you ever wonder how that whole 'doing it yourself' thing even got started? I don't even remember how I learned it. That would be kind of cool if we learned it in school and your vice principal tapped you on the head with a hammer just hard enough to let you retain the knowledge but forget the lesson.

Could you imagine if the teacher took five guys on a field trip to the lavatory? He lines you up in front of the urinals…

"Okay boys, your daddy may have taught you how to ride a bicycle but today, I'm gonna teach you something you're gonna like forever. Ready? Drop trow!" (*sigh*) "Pull your pants down, morons."

"MR. BATOR!!!"

"Show me your johnson, Johnson!"

Slowly five pairs of denims start to fall.

"Okay…with your right hand reach over and grab your unit. Be sure you grab your unit and not somebody else's. That could result in your teeth being knocked out.

"Okay, you see what happened there? You woke him up. Now he'll just kinda jump around. Alright, now tighten your grip. Now you don't want it too loose or your weasel may get away. But also, not too tight. You don't want his little tongue to hang out. Your face is turning purple, Johnson! That's too tight!"

Student: "Does it really have a tongue?"

Mr. Bator: "Go ahead and squeeze Johnson, and you tell me."

Student: "OOWW…no, it doesn't."

Mr. Bator: "Okay, now you want a nice smooth back and forth rhythm…that's right. It's somewhere between a ballet move and starting up a chainsaw."

Student: "OOWW."

Mr. Bator: "What's the matter now, Johnson?"

Student: "Too much chainsaw."

Mr. Bator: "Okay, now imagine if a girl you like was doing the pulling for you…"

(*All students screaming*)

Mr. Bator: "Stop screaming! That's supposed to happen. That lets you know you are finished. Are there any questions…Johnson?"

Student: "Wanna buy my bike?"

Mr. Bator: "Before you go back to class stop off at Vice Principal Wacker's office. He has something for you."

Student: "A diploma?"

Mr. Bator: "Sure, Johnson. Whatever you want."

———

That's probably why most people drink – to forget non-alcoholic weirdness and replace it WITH alcoholic weirdness. But with all the problems alcohol causes, I'll bet it's been a cure a great many times.

There was one time I was in a restaurant in Hawaii and I was sitting at the bar getting loaded. I mean, LOADED! So I turn around to look over the place and my eye catches sight of this gorgeous Italian girl sitting at a table all by herself. GODDESS…and I can't help but 'eye bang' her. She was just gorgeous. My eyes were making mental pictures of her and filling an album; my imagination was photo shopping her naked, in my bed.

So as I'm gawking at her, I can feel myself being watched. Five seconds later somebody brings me back to reality by tapping my shoulder.

"Hey man, what are you looking at?"

I'm not thinking at this particular moment, so I reply, "That beautiful woman in the green dress. That's the kind of woman I'd like to die on top of. Life will not get any better than the five seconds of pleasure a woman like that can give to you."

He says, "That's my wife."

I stand up and shake his hand, sniffing his fingers discreetly. Then I buy him a shot of Jack. Ten minutes and five shots later he's giving me incredibly descriptive details of their honeymoon. She was a virgin the first night and a total freak by Monday. He said nothing offended her and she was up for anything.

That was fifteen years ago and I **still** resurrect her image when I need…you know…squirt squirt. That's probably why I like Jack so much; one taste and I think of my girl.

————

The mind is a funny thing. I was friends with a guy who died of AIDS. After he died, for whatever reason, anytime I'd 'do it myself,' my brain would put a condom on my fantasy. Yeah. Halfway through foreplay my imaginary girlfriend would look up at me and hand me an imaginary condom.

By the way? Nothing kills the mood faster than one of the kids banging on the bathroom door while putting on an imaginary condom.

Chapter 6:
Toys for the Mind

Going native on a chemical vacation.

A weird feeling overtakes you when you meet Mr. Green. With a pen in my right hand, I flicked the pocket clip. The vibration is very quick, maybe a second in time. A shot of electricity shoots up my arm and through my head, then down both arms. It's almost like thinking with another man's brain. I can also choose to slow all that I feel down for a flash. It's simply a matter of bending a note of an electric pulse. Visually, it's possible too. I can look at a wall but not see it. In my mind, I can see whatever I want. I see without eyes.

If I want to see a rose, I can. So strong a vision, I can even smell it. The brain is the greatest toy that I know. You can play with it, blindfold it and shut it down for just a bit. You do have to hope you can wake it up and not realize it can shut **you** down at any time.

That is called *stalling*. And only if you're stoned would you understand what has just transpired.

Your brain is alive.

———

Do you know there are people out there with you tonight that have never gotten high? I know…can you believe that? I mean 'pot' high. Drunk is drunk, coke is coke and acid is…WOW. Like a living cartoon, man.

I mean, just sit there and smoke a whole joint then go, 'WOOOO.' I'll tell you how it is, just so you know.

First you smoke. Then…you know that voice in your head? Currently, I have three and they are all bastards. But you know **the** voice, right? Whether you know it or not, it is constantly chattering away at you all day long. Most people can shut it out but it's always there.

Well…this voice gets louder and you tend to realize he or she has a lot to say. And the first thing your voice will say is, "Oh my god, I can really hear myself. Everything seems so clear. I like this. I wonder if there's any ice cream left."

So once you find the ice cream, the first thing you notice is that it's faster to eat it out of the container than actually putting it in a bowl.

And you might giggle when your mind says 'bowl.'

So you'll eat…and eat…and no matter how much ice cream is in the container, it's not enough. Now here is where a beginner can have a bout of paranoia. You might think there is no more ice cream *anywhere* in the world, and it's very sad. Then you will go out to the kitchen again and find that unopened box of Oreos and pray for some milk…the party is on again.

Your voice is still jabbering in the background, "Okay, that's enough. Don't want to eat them all. Okay, maybe just one more…"

This can go on for a while.

If you're going to do this on any kind of semi-regular basis, you'll learn to get snacks *before* you smoke...it's all about practice.

Your activity list is varied. Some people love doing things like housework, yard work. But, most people? No work. A lot of people like sex or TV when they're high. One or the other. Most can't handle both at the same time, "Oh baby, you feel so...HEY! Is that Porky Pig? Oh, I love this one."

So...choose.

And you only do this if you have a couple hours to kill. If you're a doctor and you are doing a bowel resection that day, you may want to leave that joint in your locker till later. Nobody likes a giggling surgeon. Or a surgeon who's trying his sense of humor out on a patient before he goes under:

"Are these the breast implants you ordered, Sir?"

"Don't worry we'll have that gerbil out in one minute."

"Is it the left leg or the right leg that's coming off? I can't read the writing on the chart."

So...just wait.

And, unfortunately – no matter what your goal was – you're not going to go insane, kill anybody, or accidently drink Clorox.

After you're done eating then watch a couple episodes of "South Park." This life of debauchery usually leads to a nap. *Ooooohh, scary.*

Then when you wake up you'll probably forget you got high, but wonder why there's Doritos cheese on your fingers.

Congratulations! You are now one of us.

———

Know what? I have a truth streak a mile wide. And it gets worse when I get high. Do you know how hard it is for me to lie to a cop when I'm high?

Cop: "Mr. Morgan, have you been smoking pot?"

Me: "Yes, but it's medicinal."

Cop: "Oh, I'm sorry. Glaucoma?"

Me: "No. I was just bored. I feel much better now…or at least I did."

I'm a terrible liar when I'm drunk. A child could catch me in a lie when I'm drunk.

Child: "Have you been drinking?"

Me: "Hell no."

Child: "How many drinks did you have?"

Me: "About 7 or 8…*Damn it*!"

I don't lie when I'm on cocaine, but only because I can't talk. My lips are saying one thing and my voice is saying another. Then I just stutter like a babbling brook. "Heba duba Yuba Doba." Like Mushmouth from "Fat Albert."

When I was getting ready to go to my 25th year class reunion, I had a dream that I spiked the punch bowl with acid just to see who could still 'hang.' That was a cool dream; lots of colors. And when I woke up and relived it, I had to convince myself that it was a bad idea. That would be 'hell' night.

We did that to each other in high school all the time. One time I put a hit of acid on a friend's water ice when he wasn't looking. He figured it out by the time he was done.

Friend: "Dude, you dosed me?"

Me: "Yeah, haha."

Friend: "But I have a karate tournament in an hour."

Me: "Sucks to be you, dude."

And I walked away...

Dosing people builds character.

———

For part of my show I always try to throw a little bit of helpful knowledge at you guys as a special way of saying 'Thanks' for being here.

So tonight's spot of helpful information is: "How to help yourself survive a bad trip."

Now as most of you know, with a good trip you're just floating in wind that's not really there. You feel like you just drift from place to place. And if you ever decide to look down and watch the mechanics of your legs in motion, you'd be amazed. You're like, "Wow man…I'm mobile."

And you can wiggle your fingers in front of your face for hours and be entertained. Yes, that's the good trip. *It's a lot more fun than it sounds.*

With a bad trip you can melt into the fibers of your sofa and not be able to get up. That's not good. Before we go any further on this subject, there are ways to avoid bad trips.

Don't do acid on an airplane. *That doesn't even sound good on paper.* If you need to take a walk or some fresh air, you're boned. And that's bad. Hence the name, "bad trip."

Doing acid in jail is never a good idea. Somebody asks you for a smoke and you're watching purple fur growing out their eyeballs. That has the possibility of ending badly too.

And keep away from heights, deep water and fire. Other than that, it's a lot of fun.

But if you think your mind is going to turn around and attack you, you need to get that thought out of your head. An out of control mind is a danger because the thought process can spin off into overload and you can *really* go into a bad freak out.

What you want to do is eat something…other than more acid. And nothing larger than the size of half a grape. I don't want to be responsible for someone choking on a Hershey's Kiss. You know what? Just get a drink and then play music you really like. You can turn your day of hell into heaven with just three chords and a lot of volume.

…And a joint could help.

Speaking of pot…*again* – I can kill two birds with one stone. I can go on *match.com* and where you put what you're looking for in a woman, write: "a valid medical marijuana card."

I'm willing to lower my standards for a valid card.

JUST LEGALIZE IT ALREADY!

———

The idea of legalizing pot freaks a lot of people out. It would probably be like a big shock at first and then after a while it'd be normal. Like the first time a woman puts on clothes and guys are like, "Hey, whoa…what are you doing over there? Don't do that."

After a while it was just normal. We didn't like it, but what are you going to do?

I often wondered, well…obsessed over what would happen if other leaves got you high? Say, pine needles? Just suppose you had a handful of pine needles, splashed some vodka on them then let it dry. You smoked it and got high. Would they chop down every pine tree? Stop selling vodka? Cancel Christmas? Is that what they'd do? You have no idea how far your government will go to prevent you from enjoying certain 'journeys of the imagination.'

I smoked a maple leaf once. *I had to, my dealer was late.* No 'journey,' but I got a sore throat. But what if it HAD worked and I put it on the internet? The world would change overnight...Canada would be considered cool. All *kinds* of crazy things like that.

You know what? After twenty years I finally developed my own kind of drug; it's a mixture of crushed up Viagra and cocaine. This way, when I'm snorting coke, I can do more than just...snort coke. I think I'll call it 'Gateway.' Try to take some of the heat off marijuana.

That'd be so cool if pot was legal and became as socially acceptable as alcohol. You could walk around your garden before work with your psychedelic watering can:

"Hi Phil."

"Hey Charley. Nice buds."

"Thanks. You too."

...You'd go to a regular bar to get beer and some wings, or go to a pot bar for a joint and a pizza with Cocoa Puffs.

...Restaurants would start putting smoking sections in instead of taking them out.

...McDonalds would have a smoking section. "I'll take the 'Extreme Happy Meal for Adults,' and a coke."

...Ah...that's the life!

———

A couple years before my dad died, we were at a bar drinking beer and he asked me what the first drug was that I ever abused. I gave it some thought and replied, "ex-lax and Kaopectate...I used to wash down the ex-lax with Kaopectate, actually."

So my dad's staring at me, just wondering what else could possibly come from the lips of his oldest son. I didn't disappoint...

"So, after a couple days I had a bowel movement and it came out as little rabbit turds...millions of little rabbit turds."

So my dad says, "And that got you high?"

"No, but it felt good pooping."

I recommend it but I don't guarantee it. Results may vary…**comprende?** I am not telling you to try it…but if you do, let me know how it works out for you. I like scientific feedback.

———

When I'm not getting high, alcohol will do.

Beer after work on Friday is the best, isn't it? A couple pitchers of golden hops and those last forty hours of slavin just melt away. I love beer. Once I start with a beer buzz, I just wanna keep going till I close the bar or I run outta money.

And that's one of two problems I have with drinking. Another is my tolerance for somebody rambling on and on about some dumbass event in their life. Then they'll repeat certain parts over and over and over again. I'll let them talk, on and on, and as they keep flapping their gums, in my mind I'm fantasizing their demise. It's like gymnastics for my imagination. I have to, or I'll show boredom.

Usually, it will have something to do with the speaker's head. Like a spider with cobras for legs, descends down its little web. The cobras violently attack their nose, biting it multiple times, while the spider body has sex with their retinas. Or something more simple, like a jackhammer working over the center of their head. Just…'bang, bang, bang!' Know what? I've fantasized about that one so often I think some people have actually felt it. They begin to scratch…I take that as a victory.

If you're gonna rape my ear, I'm gonna make you itch!

I don't think I understand beer boundaries yet. If someone comes over I offer them a beer.

"You want a beer? Okay, how bout after your pancakes?"

You know what's better than beer though? FORBIDDEN beer. Remember when you were a kid hanging out with your friends and you go over to one of their houses and creep into their basement with the 'secret' refrigerator? One of your friends quickly grabs a beer and you run like a bunch of assholes out the backdoor. Then you race to somebody's fort and crack that bitch open. It might even be a stinkin *Schlitz* extra lite, but it was great because that was FORBIDDEN beer.

Now, **that** was living.

I still do it with my friends. We love FORBIDDEN beer. Of course, the 'plans' to achieve FORBIDDEN beer status have become a lot more complex.

Now, I'll go to a house like I'm going to buy it with a couple of my friends. As the realtor is walking me around, one of the guys will hang back and clean all of the beer out of the fridge and place it in his pockets. Then he'll walk back to the car and transfer it to our ice-filled cooler. Then the rest of us run back to the car, leaving the realtor with his jaw just a-hangin.

That's *good beer.*

I know I'm fifty, but that's the one bad thing I like to do.

…Huh…I just realized I've been drinking Forbidden beer for six decades. Who knows? Maybe I **am** an asshole.

I was looking for a house last year – you know, to buy. And it's important to bring some tools with you. I take a screwdriver, a flashlight…and a jacket with huge pockets. That's just in case the pictures in the realtor's office were deceiving and the place is a real shithole. That house will be missing beer, so don't waste my fucking time!

I also bring some friends with me for a couple of reasons: To make sure I don't make any snap decisions. *I might buy a house because of the pool but half the roof might be missing.* And so we can discuss which room will be the best for the 'party' room. It's gotta be big enough for a pool table, a ping pong table and the bar. The TV's not important; they're so skinny nowadays that I can nail it to the ceiling if I have to.

And you **have** to bring the right friends. I bring the "Jim Boys."

Skinny Jim likes the buzz he gets when he licks electrical outlets, so he goes around and checks all the outlets for me.

Fat Jim checks the plumbing. At almost 400 pounds, if he can't crack a toilet then it will surely hold my skinny little ass. Then he'll test the water pressure with a ten-pound 'movement.' Again, if his 'nugget' don't clog the neighborhood's main sewer line, I might put a bid in. If nothing else, they like FORBIDDEN beer too.

———

Have you ever heard of a dry town? I can *understand* a dry town. You don't want your citizens to drink and reap all the tax dollars that come with that…Fine! What I don't get are the places that let you buy it six days out of seven, with the 7th day being illegal. WHY?

Isn't there something about that in the Constitution? I think it goes: Freedom of Speech, Bearing Arms, and Beer Seven Days a Week.

What are you supposed to do if you get drunk at your house and then run out of beer? Call a cab to take you to the next state where you grab a six-pack and come back? That one six-pack will cost you $103 plus tip!

I'll bet there's a speakeasy in a bunch of basements in these towns. You rap on the door and hit them with a password:

"Charlie is a Tuna."

Then a tough mug lets you in and a flapper girl tries to sell you a pack of smokes.

So you go to the bar and order a drink. And it don't matter what you order, it all tastes like gin and turpentine. Strangely, everything is in black and white.

But those six-day towns suck. Like going to a sports bar and getting ready to watch the kickoff…

Me: "Bartender, I'd like one of those insanely large beers, two double shots of Jack, a Black Russian and a Screwdriver. And deliver each one at two-minute intervals."

Bartender: "We have Coke or Mountain Dew."

Me: "But…all the stuff is sitting there, three inches from your hand."

Bartender: "Yeah, but we're not allowed to sell it. We could lose our license."

They love saying that.

Me: "But…but I…"

Bartender: "Coke or Mountain Dew?"

Me: "I guess Coke is like…*Coca Cola*?"

Bartender: "Yes, sir."

———

I probably would not have handled prohibition well at all. I had a little taste of it this year and it sucked.

I was about 150 miles away from this three-day barbeque down south when my car broke down in the middle of this little town. I won't say what town because I eventually cursed the hell out of it.

Luckily, we were close to a gas station so we pushed it. The mechanic was just going home, said he'd fix it in the morning and pointed to a motel across the road.

Me, my girl and the lone six-pack got a room. Ten minutes later the six-pack was gone and we are revved up to party. We ask the guy in the motel office, "Where is the nearest bar?"

"9 miles that way"

"Really?" I said. "Well, how about a liquor store?"

He said, "It's across the street from the bar."

So now I'm thinking… no car… 9 *miles*? "Is there a cab around here?"

He said, "Yeah, but the only driver died six years back." Then he said, "This is a dry town."

"What the hell does *that* mean?"

"We don't allow alcohol in this town."

I just looked at him a moment and laughed, "Dude…you almost had me with that one. Come on, where's the bar?"

But he was serious. It took me a couple of minutes to realize that he wasn't pulling my chain. So I thought some more, "Can you get me some pot?"

Dude: "No."

Me: "Cocaine?"

Dude: "No."

Me: "Mushrooms?"

Dude: "YES."

Me: "Magic?"

Dude: "Oh…no."

We got half a dozen cans of whipped cream and ended up with some kind of Freon buzz. Once I start thinking about partying…I'm not easily distracted.

By the second week of Prohibition, my still would have been up and running.

Oh, and that party/barbeque I was going to ended up to be another "End of the World" party.

I love this age we live in. Every couple years some ancient calendar tells us that our world is coming to an end. And I have the type of friends that think that's good enough for a big ole' mother of a party.

A truckload of beer, a pound of weed and cases of assorted foods for the grill. But no milk and bread; we'll leave that crap for the wusses. If this world splits in two and we get sucked into a black hole, my people are leaving this planet laughing their asses off and singing, "Highway to Hell."

That would be something. Me and my drunken friends meeting the Lord together.

Saint Peter holding me up, "And **this** one climbed over the gate."

"I'm sorry, Lord. I did the same thing at the White House and Graceland. By the way, if I throw up off this cloud can I guide it to where I want it to go? I forgot to say goodbye to someone."

I'll bet dying really kills your buzz.

Chapter 7:
Conglomafux II: Rise of the Conglomafux

There are people sitting there with you right now who are dumb as a stump. And if you're thinking, "Well that's not politically correct," YOU are who I'm talking about. I've had it up to my freakin eyeballs with people diving out of other people's way so they don't offend them.

There are people out there actually trying to get the word "God" taken off our money! *I'll be passing around a plate later so if you're offended by your money, I'll be happy to take it off your hands.*

I'm offended that you're offended. We're even! Now go back to your little group of fuckbubbles and try to be more productive.

I know some of you folks are a little slow in the head. And you probably don't even realize it. You probably think you're as swift as everybody else but the rest of us know better. We can spot you in a crowd.

I better explain. There are people that do things or wear things in order to be different but it doesn't work. I'm not talking about individualism – that's cool. Invent something and make it your own. I have *my* own thing. I shake hands left-handed to start a new, healthier trend. Why? Because I know what guys do with their right hand…you know, in the bathroom (yank, yank).

And I also know that most guys don't wash their hands when they leave the bathroom. If the mood hits me in a public bathroom when a guy goes from the toilet to the door without washing, I'll say, "Are you fucking allergic to soap?" Of course, some guys *are* left-handed, but the 'essence of other guy pinga' ratio drops dramatically. Call it my little contribution to hygiene.

———

I was in the mall at the food court eating my first Mc Rib sandwich of the season when a woman in spandex walked by. *The story goes downhill from here, folks.* She had to weigh 450 pounds. If you're 7 foot 6, that's probably a *little* heavy, but she wasn't 7 foot 6; she was probably closer to 4 foot 6. There were so many dimples on her ass it looked like a cupcake pan...*YUCK.* And the pink thong glowed through this white, yet very durable fabric.

I was fat for a while. Know what I did? I covered up so people could eat their McRib sandwiches without being grossed out. Luckily, I had the munchies so I ate it, but I was close to throwing it out.

See, marijuana cures. Therefore, I am not only hygienic but also a problem solver.

———

I love working out problems, especially if it helps during the day. People see you in a new perspective, and you never lose another argument again.

The Wife: "Are you sure those dishes are clean?"

You: "Why, they far exceed my rigorous standards."

See? You sound like you're really on top of things.

The Boss: "Dump those trash cans faster."

You: "If we slow down, we can earn overtime."

You can revolutionize the world with thoughts like that.

A Comic on Stage: "Hey slick, are you gonna butter up the old noodle later on tonight?"

You: "No, your mother's waiting for me in the backseat of my car."

See? It never hurts to have a couple 'your mother' jokes on standby.

———

I just found a new, favorite bumper sticker. "No good deed shall go unpunished." I'm not sure what it means but I think it has something to do with marriage. "The way to a man's heart is through his stomach." No, but you're close. A little farther south... southier... oops...and there's the South Pole.

When I got older I realized what my pinga really was. It's a leash, and I like to be dragged around by it all day. Isn't it ironic that the only people who say, "Beauty is only skin deep," are ugly people? Up yours, Uggo!

Speaking of sex...

———

I just realized I've never had sex outside in the rain. Huh...so I haven't done it everywhere yet.

I think I have a bit of narcolepsy...no, wait...narcissism. That thing where you think you're kinda cute? Your momma told me I was damn cute, and I tend to believe your momma. Your momma... *see*? Always come in handy.

Just a rhetorical question here: Did you ever go to the mall and compare your looks against everybody else you look at?

"Better than you…Better than you…oh my, *much* better than you. I hope you don't give me nightmares." And as you're thinking this last one, he stops walking and looks right at you. I don't know if it was E.S.P. or I was just talking out loud…again.

Am I a bad person? Should I love everyone?

I think I'm getting cynical. I can't imagine an honest politician. Can you imagine one turning down a bribe? "Keep your dirty money. I work for the people! Just kiddin. Give me the briefcase."

I would love to develop a great loving attitude toward all the politicians of this country. I would love to pay our politicians even more than they grossly overpay themselves because I know they are working hard to make a better life for me. I would love to do all of that…but I can't.

It boggles the mind that our government has shut itself down more times than any other government. How spoiled do you have to be that you can walk out on your job knowing it will be there tomorrow? Why am I bringing this up? Because I saw two waitresses going at it in a Starbucks; and I mean hair pulling and booby punches. Three minutes later they were making cappa…cappuc…coffee, side-by-side.

I think some of those Asian governments are like Starbucks. Did you ever see one of their debates? Somebody disagrees and a barrage of cheap plastic chairs fly around the room. I just saw another one on TV. I forget if it was the news or "America's Funniest Videos." I laughed a lot, but that's no indication.

Know what I always thought was funny? I don't know if every baby does this, but when my kids were babies they would just stop and look straight ahead as they filled their diaper. They'd be crawling around and babbling over everything they see. In mid-crawl, they would stop like a pointer showing the hunter where the duck is…and if you were quiet, you could hear it. Yes, your babies' bowel movement. Get the camera! It almost sounds like cement coming out of a cement mixer.

Then they continued on with their present activity, not even giving a thought to what just happened. A baby is not disgusted by anything. The couple times I, as an adult, had a 'juice fart' I was completely grossed out. I don't care what fast food joint I had to stop at, one of their bathroom trashcans was going to house a pair of my underwear…soiled. *I'm sorry.*

I forget how I went from our government to discarded, encrusted underwear…but there are probably a million scenarios to get there quite easily.

Do you know when we'll find out what our government is worth? When Doomsday comes, we'll see. They say it's coming, but who 'they' are I have no idea. But there are a lot of people buying into this whole Doomsday thing in December 2012, and they *all* have their little groups.

You have the **survivalists** – they have the underground bunker sealed in lead, chock full of machine guns and cans of tomato soup. If you're betting, these guys are the heavy favorites to survive…hence, the name.

Then you have the – for lack of a better term – the **knuckleheads**. They're buying shit they don't need that doesn't require a payment for the first year. I think these folks are going to be the most surprised at the New Year's Rockin' Eve Party.

After them you have people like me who think…YAY! Another reason to have a party.

"Merry Christmas, Happy New Year and, Oh, Shit! The Anti-Christ!"

———

I guess the *Ultra-Religious* would come next; they're split down the middle. Half are desperate to save my soul and the other half is waiting to watch my soul grow crispy in the lakes of fire. Cool!

Then there is a group that understands the fact that they're *supposed* to believe an Apocalypse, and when nothing happens, they're waiting to jump out and scream, "We told you so!" We'll call them the *Asshole* group.

Then there's the *D.K.D.C's* – "Don't Know, Don't Care's." I think I can swing a few of them over to the 'party' side.

I'm sure there are a lot more cynical groups out there. All I know is that if the world blows up I'm flying through those Pearly Gates with a bottle of Jack in my hands. "Breakout the shot glasses, Lord. I'm coming home." (*Even the choir should get into that!*)

―――――

Get your life in order, folks. Set yourself some easy goals. When I was young, I thought I was setting simple, easy goals for myself. Man, I had no idea...

Goal #1: "Have a beer in every country!" *I thought, how hard could that be?* Well, turns out you need a passport, a destination, oh yeah, and a shithouse load of money. There are 191 countries…I think. I'm halfway through life and I'm stalled at…2. Yeah, here and Tijuana, and I've heard Tijuana doesn't count. So, I'm stuck at one country, unless twelve miles from land on a boat counts. *It doesn't?* Okay, then only the one.

I'd like to at least make it to my E.H.C.: That's, <u>Ethnic Heritage Countries</u>. Pretty good, huh?

I think the first place would be Germany. Sit around drinking Germany's 20-proof ale, listening to oompah loompah bands and wondering if my waitress can kick my ass. They can do that, you know.

And after four or five good hangovers, I want to go to a market and ask an authentic German butcher the eternal questions nobody else has the guts to ask. "Why are all your meats in the shape of a pinga?" *It is. It's all…tube shaped; liverwurst, bratwurst, gopherwurst.* Is 'wurst' German for pinga? That would make for strange pillow talk. "Gee Hans, your wurst is the best."

I love the Germans. They're crazy. And it would be a whole different world if Hitler's daddy had put his foot up lil' Adolf's ass a few times. He was probably a 'time-out' child: "Stop bothering the little Epstein boy, Adolf. Come here…snell…eins…zwei…Don't let me get to drei or dare be no Wiener Schnitzel for you tonight!" *Nobody would have ever even heard of Hitler if he had a stutter…*

A.H.: "Yavites lest a br br broning to da vi vi vitunhumol… ach ach ach to leber hymd…"

Crowd: "Who **is** dis dumkoff?"

––––––

I'd like to go to Germany and celebrate Christmas; me as the Burgermeister Meisterburger, but not this year. This year I'm designing a special Christmas tree – 7 feet tall and so wide. And every Christmas ball will say 'Merry Christmas.' And I have a cool little ball that has a little penguin that waddles out from his igloo and says, 'Merry Christmas,' then goes back home.

I also have a small figurine of two elves holding a flag that reads, 'Merry Christmas.' I even have garland, and every foot says, 'Merry Christmas.' The lights blink to the song, 'White Christmas.' And sitting on top is a white star with Christ on a cross in the middle and on his arm is tattooed a sleigh that reads, 'Merry Christmas.' Over top of the tree I'm gonna hang a huge banner that reads, 'Merry Fucking Christmas.'

Then I'm having two parties; one for normal friends and family. Don't worry I'll take down the banner. The second party is for my 'friends' who would find it all very 'offensive.' These are people you deal with but don't have to like, like.

Like my 'friend,' Jeff. He thinks it's a 'holiday' tree and the word 'God' should be taken off money. If it wasn't for the fact that he sells the best pot in town I'd never talk to the creep…uh, my friend. I'll listen to his five minutes of Mumbo Jumbo if he gives me a heavy count. *That's street lingo…go ask a teen.*

See? I bring people together.

And Phyllis, one of my agents – she went to an airport last year to protest. So there were no Christmas decorations when I got home on the 23rd. It was very depressing but she makes me money; I'd throw a cup of urine at her if she didn't keep finding me work.

I have half a dozen of these kinds of personality deformities circling my orbit. I probably have more but they are smart enough to be quiet about it. I'm not crazy about the Easter Bunny but most people like him so I don't say anything about it. Why should I pee on your parade? It's not like I don't like the Easter Bunny but why, you know, a *rabbit*? What is the connection between the most famous person of his time being murdered and a candy dealing rabbit? Show me the connection better than "South Park's" and I'll be fine with a rabbit. But until then…

So…my party, I'll steer those people into the living room after they have a couple drinks. Then I'll make a big deal about the tree. "Look, every ball says 'Merry Christmas.' Isn't that nice?" Hope you all like Bing Crosby.

And everybody will be biting their lip. Nobody will say anything because they all make good money off me – and you can't insult your 'Golden Goose.' I may stop laying golden eggs. I might get stage fright, writers block, or decide to clean out my system.

And then I'd have to push the envelope. I'll shake everyone's hand and say 'Merry Christmas.'

"Merry Christmas, Jeff."

"Yeah, you too, Buff."

"Say it Jeff…or I'll do something 'erotic' to your next eggnog."

"Happy?"

"NO."

"Okay...Merry Christmas."

"Very good."

———

Why do people think they can just screw around with everybody's traditions? In the 60's everyone did their own thing, quietly.

The Jewish people? You wouldn't see them for a week. They'd be hanging out with a cool looking candelabra, with a big sign over the local deli that read, "Happy Chaka Khan." Then, in the 70's, it was "Kwanza." Again, I have no problem with it, but really, how do you spell it? Every year I'll see three or four different spellings of it, but...I'm happy if you're happy.

I Google'd the strangest Christmas traditions last year and some folks are *really* out there. I watched one video where a guy's aunt would get drunk and go out in the barn and milk the bull...*No, I said bull*. That makes as much sense as the Easter Bunny. I'd love to see that connection.

Know what? Going to the circus is like a holiday. When I go to the circus I really like the clowns. I know, right? They're like mimes on acid. Always stuck in an invisible box, or pulling on a rope that isn't there, or tripping over their huge feet. You never know what kind of personality is behind the makeup. Are they someone that's short a few chromosomes ready to snap, or just a frustrated actor trying to make a living?

From a non-clown perspective, I'd hate to be killed by a clown. There's just no way to make that sound good in the papers…"Comic killed by clown." That kind of humiliation can follow you into your next life.

"Hey, aren't you the guy that got killed by a clown in your last life? What a shmuck."

I never considered being a clown. I just never wanted to wear a polka-dotted suit and gyrate in people's faces. Who'd have thought there's earning potential there?

But, getting back to holidays…

———

Holidays are always nice when they come, and usually better when they go. And sometimes you're not sure what the holiday means…exactly.

Take Valentine's Day. Is that love for your partner, or love for everybody? And is it love of the heart, or is it hard, physical rug-burn love? Ugly slapping time? Fifty Shades of Happiness? If **that's** the case, forget the flowers and candy. How about a Viagra and some wine? That combo would make it a *great* holiday.

That's the greatest thing about Viagra. If *you're* too busy to think about having sex, it's still the first thing on his mind. You can be giving her the night of her decade and your mind is a hundred miles away thinking about the stats of your dream team. Viagra ranks right up there with the invention of the wheel.

As I stated before, one of my favorite holidays is St. Patrick's Day. Aahh, those crazy Irish. It's a celebration of the day St. Patrick rid

Ireland of all the snakes. Personally, I don't think there were any snakes on the whole fuckin; island, but if that's a reason to drink, it's good enough for me.

Some people think the Irish and drinking is an ugly stereotype, but I say it ain't. The most profitable invention credited to the Irish is the bottle opener. Even their state bird is a bottle of Wild Turkey.

When I think of the 4th of July it's not all about fireworks and barbeques to me. It's the rebellious spirit of our forefathers. I can see them all standing there, on a beach at the Jersey Shore, giving the finger to England. "Tax this, bi-otch!"

England really thought they could control us from way over there...*So* wasn't gonna happen.

"What's that, England? We can't smoke pot here? Well, we're gonna. We're gonna smoke it. We're gonna make rope out of it. And we're gonna put it in our salads. Damnit, it's what's for dinner!"

The Eisenhower years took that simple pleasure away from us in the fifties…bastards!

Halloween, as a kid, was my favorite. You controlled your destiny. You can walk in a nice tight little group, or you can run from house to house and really clean up. I had candy till Christmas. When my friends finished their candy in a week I'd come in like a dealer, sucking up lunch money.

"Hey Jimmy. Could I interest you in a Baby Ruth bar?"

I was the only seven-year-old on my block with my own accountant.

———

Thanksgiving was just a big meal; our family just went along with the program. Everybody cooks a turkey this day, so will we. If anything, I'm offended being part American Indian. That's right. To us, it's more of a *last* meal.

"Take a drumstick and get the fuck out."

There was no co-existing here. "We want you to stop your happy way of life and communing with nature to join our rat race, or…we shoot you."

They probably didn't get the "F.U." out of their mouths before they were eating musket balls.

The spirit of Christmas! The giving and warm feelings toward the people you tolerate on a daily basis. "I can't stand Joe but I still have to get him a tie." Christmas is only fun if you have money to buy people presents. If you just sold the last pint of blood the hospital was willing to take, you maxed out at the sperm bank and your shopping Christmas Eve at the dollar store…Christmas sucks. If you have to go to a cemetery to pick up flowers for your honey, Christmas sucks. If you ever glued together Popsicle sticks to make your presents, Christmas sucks.

That's why people drink during the holidays. Alcohol makes things look better than they really are. "Wow! Beer coasters made from Popsicle sticks? Thanks, Dave!"

If you take New Year's right down to its essence, it would sound like this: "Hey, I'm hanging my new calendar, anybody wanna party?"

Then the kegs and Dick Clark arrives. *(Well...now we have to deal with that Ryan Seacrest idiot, but Dick will always arrive in my drunk, happy head!)*

People just go nuts over new calendars...

———

Oh crap, I forgot. I need a lawyer.

I have a legal question I'd like to ask a lawyer if there are any out here tonight. One...two...wow, three lawyers here tonight! Watch your step when you leave, I'm not sure the owner is insured. *You know how lawyers can be.*

Say, what was it that got you guys so anxious to come here tonight that you took out a crowbar and ripped twenty bucks out of that scarcely used wallet of yours? Has to be a woman…or a man.

Yeah, you got that I'm not a lawyer - friendly, huh? Lawyers are actually the reason the country is in such bad shape – you pulled the top spot away from the government.

Hey, what do you call 100 lawyers at the bottom of the ocean? That's right, a good start.

But let us put all the soft-hearted needling aside. What I want to know is, if I give my dealer counterfeit money for my weed, would I still get in trouble for the counterfeiting too if I get caught? *Really?* Well, I don't agree with you. It's a victimless crime…almost.

———

Even though I don't like lawyers, I will still circumvent the law occasionally. I believe they're called 'loopholes.' *God bless free will.*

Never underestimate the power of a good loophole. Don't you hate it when a minor celebrity name drops big celebrities they've met? That is *so* annoying.

So Gilbert Gottfried is one of my Facebook buddies. What...I'm not a celebrity? See that? **Loophole.**

So I'm writing to him and chatting with him...I have a plan. You see, I want to meet Gilbert one day...maybe become friends, you know, by hanging out with him. Maybe get drunk or stoned with him...his choice, of course. And after we get to just the right buzz...try to get him to do all the parrot scenes from "Aladdin." I love his work in that! "That's Sultan Vile Betrayer to you!"

Every line he says, I put on a wobbly marble pedestal to enjoy.

"I think I'll have a heart attack and die of not surprise." When my kids were small, we watched the shit out of that videotape...until finally, the machine ate it. We actually had a funeral for it. We each stood over it reciting our favorite parts then we buried it. And no, it wasn't my idea…entirely. And sure as hell, after that last shovelful of dirt covered the tape we were in the car to go get the D.V.D.

Gilbert Gottfried made me the great father I am today. And he doesn't even know that so don't say anything to him or he might think that's weird, or un-friend me on Facebook, and that would *so* kill my buzz. None of us wants that.

I just saw Gilbert down in Atlantic City last month. *So* funny. Now my friends go to A.C. to gamble, and I love when my friends come back with their wacky stories.

Atlantic City stories are so much different from Vegas stories. Here's a couple I've heard…

"A seagull flew over me and crapped in my open mouth. I ran to the nearest slot machine and in three spins, I won $5,000."

"I witnessed a drive-by shooting so I barricaded myself in my room. It took a small army of Spanish speaking maids two hours to get me out of there."

"I banged a hooker with a prosthetic arm. It could have been a mannequin. I was pretty drunk at the time. Hell…could have been a seagull."

One of my friends said he saw a dead body down there one time. If I ever found a dead body I think I would be devastated…unless that person died stupidly. Lots of people die stupidly.

If I come home and a burglar died trying to crawl in a window, got stuck and the outside cats are eating his carcass…I will laugh indefinitely before I call the cops.

And it wouldn't matter if it was a friend. If it's funny, I'm gonna laugh…then I'll be an adult.

If you invite me over and by the time I get there you've accidently killed yourself by auto-erotic asphyxiation, you're going up on YouTube.

Hanging by a rope, pinga in hand, I'm gonna make you a star.

There is no reason anybody should die during sex unless it's from a heart attack…that's *my* retirement plan. When self-love becomes life and death, that's when I go back to collecting baseball cards. I'm not hardcore about 'chicken chokin.'

The friend that saw the dead body is one of those 'cliché' guys; always there with a lame expression on his lips. His favorite expression is: "The Future is Now." He's always saying it when he's around me. One day I just got tired of hearing it. I turned around and said, "No…it's not! It's ahead of us. Maybe just a nanosecond, but it's ahead of us. Watch this man. I'm going to throw my arm out there and grab a piece of future. And when I bring my hand back, I just have a handful of the present. The future is the future so shut the fuck up!"

That's about the time I noticed his mom was sitting on the sofa. "Oh, hi, Mrs. Andrews, how are you doing?" Crap. *Guess* that's another Christmas card I won't be getting…I mean, holiday card.

You're not offended, are you?

OKAY, CHRISTMAS CARD!

————

The 'dead dude story' guy is pretty cool, though. He took me to a bar in the backwoods of Louisiana called "Cooter's Clinic." On paper, it's a V.D. clinic and the government pay Cooter to cure the states V-D elite. What the government doesn't know is you're more likely to catch V.D. there than actually be cured of it. This is a *real* Cajun bar. Whatever someone brings in dead off the interstate will become the happy hour buffet at 5:00 pm. *Never ask.*

And nobody really talks there; it's more like grunts. Everybody knows what everybody else is grunting about so you just kind of grunt along. It's really a higher level of communication, *it really is.*

The only thing that everyone avoids in here, besides a toothbrush (*ba-doo, bang, rim shot!*) is a bowl of potato chips. Not surprising, seeing as that the name of these chips was, "The Devil's Dick." I'm not even gonna soften it by using the word pinga. These chips were called "The Devil's Dick" for a reason.

And a crowd will gather to watch a sucker try one. If you don't cry after your first bite, you win a pitcher of beer. So I'm looking at these things and they're chocolate covered. How bad can they be?

So I pick one up and everybody starts grunting in horror. I take a bite. *Yum*…dark chocolate…wow…and cinnamon…delicious. Then I look at the bartender, "What's that third flavor? I can't identify it."

He looked at me with an insane toothless smile, "Ghost Pepper."

And in the half second it took him to say "Ghost Pepper," I pooped my pants. If there is a devil, I'm sure that's what his pinga tastes like.

That is why I have no sense of smell. But I didn't cry…I fainted.

Drugs, alcohol, weirdness…I've tried nearly everything.

————

Know what I hate about doing steroids? Nothing, I've never tried them. But what I heard is amazing. In six months, you can add 50% more muscle to your body. Now *that's* amazing. And so is the data about the one muscle that you want to grow turning into a cashew.

Know what? This is one drug I think I'll just pass on. That supersedes my entire reason to go to the gym. You know…women. I'm not bringing home women to watch *NCIS*; I want to be your favorite 'one night stand.'

I want you, on your wedding night, to think of me. I want you to wish I was showing your new husband how to make you squeal. *And for a price…I just might.* Here's a cute picture- - the Terminator using a roach clip to pee…must be tough to pee with a roach clip.

And guys have it a lot easier with the whole peeing thing. You women have your own little room, a cubicle…your own little world. If there wasn't always a line outside the ladies room (*haha*) you'd probably stay in there all day.

For men, we're just out there. We're exposed. And we're different every day. We are looked upon and judged by our fellow urinators. There are some days when you don't mind:

"Come on, Mr. Soupcan…let's try to chip the porcelain."

Then, there are days when you go all the way to the last stall. "I'm waiting for the handicap stall."

You're not lying. At that moment you feel handicapped.

"Sir, do you mind if I make one small comment about…your hygiene? I think you forgot to wash your hands when you were done, and you were in a stall, right? Well, we'll never barbeque together, I can promise you that much."

My God, how hard is that to do? I always wash my hands but I won't use the hand dryers. I know some have been used as a cheap date, and I don't want to play the odds so I avoid them all together. Paper towels or my shirt; either a tree must suffer or my shirt does. I still wonder if you can get pinga 'pets' from a toilet seat. Every couple of years the answer seems to change, like what's better for you, margarine or butter? Or Roe vs. Wade.

It's all the *Matrix* people. Nothing but deception.

———

How about all those lies they told us in school way back in the 70's? Remember? Like, soccer is gonna be bigger than baseball and football in the United States by the year 2000. *Really?* I couldn't tell you the name of two soccer players.

And there are only three things I know about soccer:

1. The ball is black and white.

2. Always bet on Brazil.

3. …nope…just two. Wait! The World Cup! That's three.

And what about the metric system? I know everything is based on 10, but if you have 9, you're screwed. The only people I know that use the metric system are soda manufacturers and coke dealers…not that I know any coke dealers…

(Smile for the camera.)

Did you notice how 'liters' never made the jump from soda to milk? We Americans made such a fuss converting quarts to liters that the metric people finally threw up their hands and said, "Fuck it!"

We really pissed them off.

My kids don't know the metric system and I always told my kids, never be afraid to ask a question. If you can't figure out your stereo system, ask questions. If you can't figure out your taxes, ask questions. …If you get invited to a sexual three-way, ask questions. Especially this one:

"So…who else is coming?"

You don't want to be surprised like those suicide bombers. They kill themselves for 72 virgins in the afterlife. 72 virgins that look just like **you**. *They're virgins for a reason, dude.*

Which brings up the question of sex after death: Unless you're a demented coroner, I don't think it exists. But I've been wrong before. Heaven might be a giant S&M den where everyone has a fetish.

"Yeah, pluck my wings…OH YEAH!"

"How the hell did you smuggle a pitchfork up here?"

"Your safe word is 'Gabriel.'"

Tell me I'm wrong…

I don't know. Maybe Heaven isn't all clouds and headboards. It *could* be a big lake, and your spirit gets its own little fishing boat.

You fish for a millennia in a fishless lake…or until you get bored watching your bobber not moving. Then you're like, "Fuck this, I'm going back to Earth."

Prove I'm wrong!

I don't think there's food in Heaven. That is going to take some getting used to. I thought of this backwards. I couldn't imagine toilets in Heaven so you can't have food there either. You can see that, right? I was hoping for weed in Heaven but I'm not holding my last breath for that one.

So…no sex, no food and no weed in Heaven. (*That's **way** worse than: No shoes, no socks, no service*). They better have one hell of a nice bowling alley up there. Otherwise, just send my ass into limbo.

I believe in Heaven but not Hell. Again, if I'm wrong, I'm not gonna be some quiet little spirit that lets the devil have his way with me; I am going to be kicking some sinner ass down there. I don't know what brimstone is but I'll be chucking a truckload of it.

Can you imagine the phone call from Satan to God?

"Hi…yeah, it's me. Hey, can you take this Buffalo guy? Well, he's really being destructive down here. Yeah, he's throwing off my torture sessions for the rest of my minions. It's like he's trying to take over. A case of beer and you'll take him? I'll make it two, big guy! Avidazen! (*German… Satan's mother tongue*)

———

But getting back to kids or even babies…is there anything cuter or funnier then when a baby learns to walk? Arms outstretched, terror in their eyes, babbling who knows what like little Frankenstein monsters. Take a couple steps…*crash*…couple more steps…*crash*.

Eventually, they get it. Then they start chasing you. The steps come a little faster and they start running, but they haven't fine-tuned their braking skills yet. As they are about to hit a wall or some other immovable object they get that 'oh crap' look in their eyes and "BAM!" they hit their face.

And you can't laugh because that kid is going to check your reaction. If you laugh, it'll cry...**a lot**. If you 'baby' it, it'll cry...**a lot**. You just have to give it a W.T.F. look and shake your head.

And **that**, Charlie Brown, is why we only use 10% of our brain. The rest is scar tissue.

Chapter 8:
And I Like You...Why?

I have two sons.

I'm glad I have two sons. I don't think I could have done that whole daughter thing. First guy that showed up for a date, I may have said something that was taken the wrong way...

"You guys go out and have a great time. I'll just stay here and sharpen my butterfly knife collection. Stab, stab, dude! I'm just kiddin...kinda."

Or how about *this* awkward conversation:

Princess: "Daddy, I got a job today. I'm gonna make $2,000 a week."

Me: "Well, just call the go-go bar back and tell them you quit, hon."

Princess: "But *daddy*! This is so unfair"

I love strippers. I'd marry a thousand of them if I could. *There may be something to being a Mormon.*

Then the inevitable happens:

Princess: "I'm getting married."

Me: "How nice. After I rob the bank on the corner we'll go talk to the caterer. Honey? Did you see my ski mask and pistol? Only the best for my little girl! Oh, yeah, and my gloves. Thank you, Honey."

I think I'm a good parent to my sons. I gave them what they needed. When they had a hard time sleeping, I'd slip 'em a couple shots of *NyQuil*. When they discovered girls, I got them a crate of condoms. And when we got the munchies…I mean, got hungry…I whipped 'em up a shrimp covered pizza.

I know what you're thinking, and I agree…I am the *coolest* dad in the world.

Being a divorced dad isn't easy though. Trying to get into a relationship with a good woman can be tough. My kids have to like her and she has to like them. That can be a pain in the ass. Yeah, and she has to be a real freak in bed…you know…sexually.

Hey, it's where I'm at in life!

Bring your spittoon.

———

But guys, when you get that special person in a relationship you have to work at it. It's not like a three day drunken sexfest where you leave the room to fart. You're there for the foreseeable future, so figure out what your stupid negative habit is and work on it.

Here's an example: A former friend of mine used to call his wife the 'c'-word when he got mad. THAT is a bad word. That word actually straightens my ass hairs.

One night, she knocked all his teeth out. Did he learn anything? No, now he calls her, "Unt."

My problem comes in the form of the 'Intention/Follow Through' syndrome. I always have the best of intentions with my girlfriend, but sometimes the follow-through sucks.

Here's an example: One night, I was talking to my talking joint…*Yes, I did. Don't judge!*

So I say to the joint, "I wonder if we have any snacks here." And the joint replies, "What about your girlfriend's unopened box of Godiva?" And I say back to the joint, "That's brilliant! Then I'll pick her up an even bigger box."

So the joint says to me, "That's a great intention…but don't forget the follow-through."

"I won't, Mr. Joint."

So I did what I did to her box of chocolates. I even licked all the little wrappers. Then I took a nap with the *full* intention of following-through on my thought. When I woke, following-through was *still* my first thought…especially with my girlfriend waving the empty box in my face, screaming, "What the fuck, man? What the fuck? I'm gone twenty minutes and you smoke the talking joint and eat *my* candy? You're like…a sick animal."

So you see how important a good follow-through is. Without that, all good intentions are just wasted promises.

_____

I do like the thought of *getting* married but actually *being* married? I don't know if I'll ever find the right one. I have strange ideas.

I want a girl I think I know, yet every once in awhile she throws me a curveball. Like, if I'm having a great day, I go home and have three or four drinks. Then she calls me up to see if I want to come over for some fun. There's nothing like having a day you'll remember the rest of your life. *That's a keeper*.

If you know ANYTHING about me, you know she has to be pot friendly. You know, loves the 'green green grass of home...'

Okay...she doesn't have to be a toker but she can't just one day come up to me and say I have to choose between the two of them. She won't like the answer. This is something I know a little something about so, yeah…*T.O.K.E.R. preferred.* I will, however, make concessions for government working candidates.

Since we're on the subject of boinking government workers, why does everyone give me crap every time I mention nailing Sarah Palin? She's pretty hot. As long as she doesn't talk during the deed, I'm sure we'll both have a great time.

———

The next subject on what it takes to make me happy…

Friends and family have their own homes for a reason. I don't want to entertain four nights a week; that's what special occasions are for.

Special occasions are just occasions if they were just held last night. There's 'us,' then there's space, then there's 'them.' The key to getting along is that nice healthy chunk of space.

And lastly…you have to talk things out. If I fucked up you have to say something NOW. You cannot collect little bits and pieces of my stupidity and one day just explode. My power of 'fact regurgitation' is roughly 18 to 24 hours. After that, it *may* have happened or could have been a dream. I just don't know.

And you don't have to look perfect, but cuteness goes a long way. Funny how it works, that whole relationship thing. Fall in love, become a parent, a grandparent, then…who cares.

But don't take life for granted. There are a lot of things you don't want to miss.

———

Guys, if you ever get a chance to watch your child being born, **do it**. It's a beautiful thing to witness the birth of your child while knowing that someday it will be half yours in the divorce settlement.

I got a double thrill. My ex was bitchin at me all through labor. I couldn't wait till childbirth. "I hope it hurts. I hope this kid weighs twenty pounds."

And as soon as the head started showing, he looked huge. I thought she was giving birth to Stewie Griffin. *I dance in your pain.*

Afterwards, the doctor told me she needed an episiotomy. You know, a couple stitches to fix her up? So I opened my wallet and flipped him a fifty. "Throw in a couple extra stitches, will ya, doc?"

Yeah…but even with a surgically enhanced scootch I just couldn't take it. We still talk…but not very often. I don't think she likes my sense of humor for some reason.

The last phone call I had with her, she was bitchin that she found a condom in our son's wallet. Our son is 19, and what she was doing in his wallet, I don't know.

So I said, "Do you expect him to be a virgin on his wedding night like you? Ha Ha Ho, baby. Come on, Honey. Laugh with me!" (*click*) "Hello? Hello?"

I love women…*most* women. Right now I'm working on a formula to get women 'in the mood'…you know, gush gush. I did figure out a formula for how to get a woman *out* of the mood. And it usually takes only eight words. Here are some varieties of the formula:

"Gee baby; those are some ugly freakin shoes."

"Yes, I think your ass is getting fatter."

"What the hell happened to your hair today?"

This formula is only to be used when you'd rather do it yourself…gush gush.

———

And another great moment in my life is coming. I've been thinking about it for years.

I can't wait to be a grandfather. But only after the kids are married…you know, like normal.

I want to know the joy of playing with someone else's kids, and when I get tired of them I can give them back.

So many people I know have experienced this beautiful and natural emotion…except me. I handed my kids out every chance I could. And whoever I gave them to would wind them up, make them go berserk and say, "Here you go." And hand them back.

I want to know **that** joy.

———

My kids and I love going to the zoo where there are always people protesting about animals in cages and having them kept outside for public display. Those animals live stress-free lives. They are well fed and have a better health plan than I do. Screw them protestors; I'd like a gig like that. And if you're a panda, the zoo people encourage you to reproduce. *Where do I sign?* That'd be great at contract negotiations:

"Okay, I want decent food, a case of rum every week and a bunch of females in my cage. No males or I don't perform."

And what would I do? I'd get drunk and have sex. Lots of sex. And all your visitors can film your little hearts out. I would be a star…and the zoo folks would be rich.

Am I full of great ideas or what? *It's a win-win-win, baby.*

———

You know, sometimes alcohol plays a hand in bad decision making. Like one time this girl dumped me and broke my heart, so I got drunk and called her. I wanted love and tenderness but got a restraining order placed against me instead.

Now this is where men and women differ. A couple years later, I broke a chick's heart. She got drunk and called me wanting one more night of passion. I said, "Sure, come on over." **That** was a great night.

A friend of mine got drunk and went on the internet. He was threatening the President, stirring up anarchy…oh yeah, and posting pictures of his pinga in various poses. "This is Johnny wearing a bagel. This is Johnny reclining on a windowsill. And this is Johnny talking on the phone to his ex-girlfriend."

The next day, my friend and Johnny got taken away by the police. Goodnight Johnny…

Me: Phil? Tell me, why did you name your pinga, Johnny?

Phil: "Well, when I was dating and it started getting physical, I'd drop my pants and say, "Heeeerrrrre's Johnny!'"

Me: "That's the stupidest thing I've ever heard."

Phil: "No. When I was dating, most girls would giggle and say that was funny."

Me: "Really?"

Phil: "Yeah, and when I started dating my wife-to-be, I did the 'Here's Johnny' thing and she said, 'Never ever say that again.' That's how I knew."

Me: "But you hate your wife."

Phil: "Yeah, so my system has a flaw in it."

Stop calling it Johnny, Phil. My god! Does that look silly? Talking to yourself? These days, you can blame it on Bluetooth. If I don't see it in one ear, I'll look in the other. I just do; I don't know why. And, sometimes, there's no Bluetooth. I'll follow *these* people through the mall. They're always so interesting.

"Oh, Cinnabons! I better not. I just did three hours on the treadmill for a slice of pizza. Well I just won't have any dinner tonight…or breakfast tomorrow. No, no! I don't need it. See? I can pass it up. I knew I could. Maybe next time…but I *did* only have a salad for lunch. Fuck it, I want one."

Then she turned around quickly, slamming right into me. I was following a little too close. *My bad. I'm such a pig.*

But that's only lust and that's different from love. Most of us are in love…to a point. You send messages like, 'love ya.' There's no 'I.' It's subsurface but not to the soul. Men, women – we're all guilty of it. It's 'Today's' love – hard and free and then it's gone.

What happened to love 'forever & ever?' or 'I'd die for you.' or 'I'll flip my dog over and you can whale on its cookies and I will still love you," that kind of true love?

Some great comedian once said, "Oral sex after twenty years of marriage is saying 'Fuck You' as you pass each other in the hall." If anybody knows who said it first, please tell me later. I'd like to send them a card. That's a great joke…when you're divorced.

Any guy in a twenty-plus year marriage right now better not even smirk at that joke. Just keep looking straight ahead like you have for twenty-plus *years*. When it gets that long, it's either pure, heavenly love…or a house of cards just…waiting.

Both of you could be like a couple of cats on acid…skitzy. Then, during one argument, that 'D' word comes out and you both look relieved.

He: "You want a divorce? I want a divorce. I've wanted a divorce for years."

She: "Oh my god. I've hated you for years."

He: "And I've hated you. You have no idea how good I feel."

She: "Yes I do. Do you have any idea how many times I've watched you sleep with a knife in my hands wishing I had the guts?"

He: "No kiddin! Hey, remember last year when you slid your car into the back of that semi and you said the brakes failed? That was me...I've been trying to kill you for years. But you're like a cat, baby...Nine lives."

She: "Oh yeah, that reminds me, the blood in your urine isn't bladder cancer. I've been spraying your food with mercury."

Oh...and if you ever do try to 'off' each other, you know the spouse is always the #1 suspect. So take some acting lessons.

Cop: "How long has your wife been gone, Mr. Morgan?"

Me: "I don't know. A week, a month, but the place hasn't been the same since she left. And no, you can't go in the basement."

———

I can prove 'love' is the work of the devil. Read the word backwards. See…you want more? Okay.

How many times has love made you want to jump off a bridge? Me? Thirty four times.

Okay, now how many times has hate made you want to jump off a bridge? See? None. Revenge, yes. Fury, yes. Mayhem, yes. But not death.

And suicide is the work of the devil. Well, that's what it said on the back of my 'Great Christians in History' collectible cards.

You need more? Okay, Valentine's is all about love. What color is your Valentine's heart? Red. In all the pictures you've seen who, exactly, is red, God or Satan?

Thank you. Thank you very much. We agree to agree.

———

Have you ever considered pimping your mate out? A little bit of a cash flow problem and the idea develops legs.

Everybody has a price. That movie, *Indecent Proposal*, Robert Redford wants to pay one million dollars to sleep with another man's wife.

I got dragged off by a woman to see it. At the end, my girl said, "You wouldn't do that to me, would you?"

(Smile) Cable bill is overdue and we're out of quarters for the Laundromat. "Have a nice time, Mr. Redford."

We **all** have a price. I have a price for most things. I'd probably bang my ex for the right price, but only if she stopped doing that one annoying thing that used to piss me off.

That 'in and out' thing…what's that called? Oh yeah, breathing. That and $50G's and we are all good.

———

I think sex is a very personal and private subject not to be taken lightly. My kids learned about sex the old fashion way…at a *Motley Crue* concert. There was a top-heavy chick, probably closing in on 40 – *in age and in bra size* – on the first level, and we were right above her on the next level. She looked real cute in her cowboy hat.

So she starts flashing both my sons - ages 14 and 13. It didn't look like it was doing them any harm so I let them have their fun. After about five or six eyefuls, she starts yelling for a dollar a flash.

So they're on me like flies on a…I mean, like flies. They caught me on a good day. I was going to a strip club after I dropped them off at home so I had A LOT of $1's.

So they start tossing dollars down to her and she just keeps her perfect pair flapping. This was fantastic. If you break it down, a dollar was a great deal. My two sons and I got a peek for a buck so that breaks down to $.33 cents a person – screw that last penny. And she had two boobs so that's $.16 cents a boob – screw that penny once again. **And** we have two eyes each, so that breaks down to $.08 cents a viewing. That's a bargain.

They don't teach that kind of math in school.

So I'm talking to my kids into making her do jumping jacks…and she did. At that moment, I loved me…my kids loved me…and every dude for five rows behind me loved me. *You just don't get that at a Justin Bieber concert.*

When we got home I put some thought into it. She was flashing and she was about 40. Okay…

She was flashing for a couple of kids that were obviously minors and she did it for singles; no $5's, $10's or $20's. *That's Rock-and-Roll, baby.*

So I guess the three greatest lessons I taught my boys were: how to ride a bike, how to fish and how to get the most out of a dollar. Yeah, and the Crue was alright, too!

———

Despite my parenting skills, my kids are pretty normal.

I loved the 'toddler' stage. Did you ever give your kid a little extra shot of *NyQuil* just so you can watch him walk into walls? No…no, just me, huh? You lying mothu…

So I guess you never made bets with your wife about when the kid will fall on his ass?

At that age, they're still getting used to their legs. At two years, the kid is still shaky and can still fall down all by themselves. An extra shot of *NyQuil* ensures a tumble or two. You can build a little obstacle course with pillows and shoes, and you make bets with each other about where 'junior' will bite the big one.

I wouldn't do it to a kid *under* two…they're still babies. That would just be bad parenting. I mean, what do I look like…a freaking animal?

Chances are he'd just cry about it anyway. They cry over everything. They'd have no appreciation of a good medicinal buzz. You can't do it for too long, though. I remember my son came home from school when he was ten and said, "Dad, my nose is running. Can I have the key to the safe to get the *NyQuil*?"

I had to lock it up then. We were going through two cases a week. But it's such a smooth buzz. When drugs and alcohol are mixed in the same bottle good things are bound to happen.

NyQuil actually saved me from being really embarrassed one night. A friend came over and he had a buzz on but I had no alcohol in the place…nothing. So I faked it.

"Hey man, wanna try a new drink?"

He agreed.

So I said, "See if you can figure out what it is."

I got a tumbler, filled it up with *NyQuil* and added a couple drops of Dr. Pepper. He had three of them and staggered home. He loved it. I'm thinking of calling it, "The Dumbass."

Watch somebody steal that idea off me and make a million dollars. If I had all the money from **all** the million dollar ideas I've had stolen from me…I'd have about $20. I'd have blown the other $10 million on *NyQuil* and whores.

Whores like *NyQuil* too, so you know it's good.

I think the *NyQuil* people ought to send me a couple of bucks for advertising the hell out of their product. People aren't going to buy it for its intended use, but what do they care? It's all about money.

So how many of you really think I guzzle *NyQuil* for kicks? Really? I am a professional entertainer...I **can** afford low-grade light beer, you know!

———

I never really dosed my kids for laughs. I've had people come up to me after shows thinking I did. Just jokes, folks. I was always helpful to my kids. Matter of fact, I just helped my younger son write a report for school.

He came home last week and asked me what the difference was between theoretical and realistic.

I said, "Go ask your mom if she'd sleep with a stranger for a million dollars."

He left and came back a minute later. "Mom said she would."

"Okay, now go ask your sister if she'd sleep with a stranger for a million dollars."

A minute later, he came back. "She said yeah too, pop."

"Okay, now theoretically we're sitting on $2 million dollars. Realistically, we're living with a couple of whores!"

Thank you…Thank you, everyone!

ABOUT THE AUTHOR

My name is Barry Hemmerle. I was a bouncer at a comedy club in the mid 1980's. Before Tim Allen broke through, we hung out together and he suggested I take a stab at comedy. After my second show, the manager thought I was good enough to M.C.

Using the name Barry Von, I worked the east coast sharpening my style of sarcastic wit. Besides jokes, I'd occasionally break beer bottles over my head or let audience members rub a spot on my temple for good luck. {It's a bullet someone put there over the beating I gave him as a teen.

A SPECIAL THANK YOU TO YOU!

On behalf of everyone at Freedom Of Speech Publishing, thank you for choosing Buffalo Morgan's Chronicles from the Asylum: Sick & Funny Comedy from Buffalo's Vegas Show for your reading enjoyment.

As an added bonus and special thank you, for purchasing Buffalo Morgan's Chronicles from the Asylum: Sick & Funny Comedy from Buffalo's Vegas Show, you can enjoy discounts and special promotions on other Freedom of Speech Publishing products. Visit www.freedomeofspeech.com/vip to learn more.

We are committed to providing you with the highest level of customer satisfaction possible. If for any reason you have questions or comments, we are delighted to hear from you. Email us at cs@freedomofspeechpublishing.com or visit our website at: http://freedomofspeechpublishing.com/contact-us-2/.

If you enjoyed Buffalo Morgan's Chronicles from the Asylum: Sick & Funny Comedy from Buffalo's Vegas Show, visit www.freedomofspeechpublishing.com for a list of similar books
or upcoming books.

Again, thank you for your patronage. We look forward to providing you more entertainment in the future.

Buffalo Morgan's Chronicles from the Asylum

Sick & Funny Comedy from Buffalo's Vegas
Show
By Barry Hemmerle

For more books like this one, visit Barry Hemmerle's
website at:
http://barryhemmerle.com/

Printed in the United States of America
The publisher offers discounts on this book when
ordered in bulk quantities. For more information,
contact Sales Department, Phone 815-290-9605,
Email:
sales@FreedomOfSpeechPublishing.com

Freedom of Speech Publishing, Leawood KS, 66224
www.FreedomOfSpeechPublishing.com

ISBN: 1938634039
ISBN-13: 978-1-938634-03-1